Writing Instruction for Generation 2.0

Gloria E. Jacobs

ROWMAN & LITTLEFIELD EDUCATION

A division of
ROWMAN & LITTLEFIELD PUBLISHERS, INC.
Lanham • New York • Toronto • Plymouth, UK

Published by Rowman & Littlefield Education
A division of Rowman & Littlefield Publishers, Inc.
A wholly owned subsidary of The Rowman & Littlefield Publishing Group, Inc.
4501 Forbes Boulevard, Suite 200, Lanham, Maryland 20706
http://www.rowmaneducation.com

Estover Road, Plymouth PL6 7PY, United Kingdom

British Library Cataloguing in Publication Information Available

Library of Congress Cataloging-in-Publication Data

Jacobs, Gloria E., 1957–
  Writing instruction for generation 2.0 / Gloria E. Jacobs.
    p. cm.
  Includes bibliographical references.
  ISBN 978-1-60709-464-7 (cloth : alk. paper) — ISBN 978-1-60709-465-4 (pbk. : alk.
paper) — ISBN 978-1-60709-466-1 (electronic)
  1. Composition (Language arts). 2. Internet in education—United States. 3. Internet
and teenagers—United States. 4. Internet literacy—United States. 5. Media literacy—
United States. 6. Digital media—United States. I. Title.
  LB1575.8.J25 2010
  428.0078'54678—dc22   2010032474

∞™ The paper used in this publication meets the minimum requirements of American
National Standard for Information Sciences—Permanence of Paper for Printed Library
Materials, ANSI/NISO Z39.48-1992.

Printed in the United States of America

DEDICATION

To Mark for his constant belief and support. To the young people who let me into their lives so that I could better understand. To the teachers who ask the hard questions.

Contents

Contents

PART III: RESOURCES

Preface: The Challenges of Teaching Generation 2.0

In the mid-1990s, as I was entering my third year as a teacher, I was asked to develop a writing course to be delivered to all ninth graders. District administrators were concerned because, according to the New York State eighth-grade English Language Arts (ELA) exam results, the district had some of the lowest scores in the metropolitan area. Despite the high visibility of the position, despite the pressure of addressing what was seen as a pressing problem, despite being not yet tenured and still trying to figure out this thing called teaching, I agreed to take on the challenge. Perhaps it was naivete, idealism, or stubbornness, but I saw this as a chance to write a curriculum that matched my beliefs about literacy learning, even if I had to hide it under the cover of increasing test scores.

I spent the spring and summer reading material on writing instruction and designing the course. It was to be a writing workshop modeled after the best of Nanci Atwell—ungraded, process oriented, and integrated with technology. I envisioned an environment in which students would feel safe and nurtured as they explored their world through writing. I imagined grammar taught in context and minilessons based on student needs. I pictured author sharing, peer workshops, enthusiastic revision and editing, and triumphant publishing parties. I dreamed of a classroom humming with activity as students tapped out inspired pieces on Internet-connected, state-of-the-art computers.

The administration gave me almost everything I wanted. Class was to be held in a computer classroom where each student would have his or her own computer linked to the Internet. The technology department provided me with a television hooked to a computer so that I could use my own writing as a model (this was before interactive whiteboards and LCD projectors were common in classrooms). A technology assistant was assigned to my room full-time so that any technological glitches could be solved immediately. I was also given a packaged writing workshop program, as well as monies with which I bought classroom sets of a writing handbook, classroom sets of a collection of short literature pieces to use as models, and other supporting materials. It was an enviable position.

Things fell apart the first week of school.

It quickly became clear that the students and I were at odds over what computers were for. I saw the computers as a tool for supporting literacy learning, and the students tended to treat the computers as a site of subversive play or as yet another roadblock in their learning. Rather than spending classroom time engaged in minilessons and one-on-one conferences, the technology support person and I became mired in a two-front battle. On one side we were wrestling with computer-savvy students who would quickly tap out an essay and then spend the rest of the time toying with the computer settings, playing games, sending e-mails, or surfing the Web for everything except what they were supposed to. On the other side we were struggling with students who needed assistance in file management, word processing, and the other basic computer skills that I (shortsightedly) had assumed all students would already be well versed in.

Computer use and the Internet remained contested turf throughout the year, but eventually I stopped fighting and remembered instead to observe, listen, and reflect on what it was my students were doing. Instead of seeing students as thwarting my efforts to teach them literacy, I began to recognize the rich literate lives that existed outside the domain of school and outside the domain of print. I struggled to find value in the online activities of my students as I realized that much of my teaching and course design was based on school-based assumptions about technology use and literacy. I also began to understand that the curriculum I had hoped would be inclusive and emancipatory actually served to marginalize some students.

This lesson of exclusion was made evident by the comments of Emma (not her real name), a girl who was new to the school. Emma had moved to the district to live with an aunt because neither her mother nor her father was able to take care of her. I felt a bond with Emma because I too lived with an aunt for a number of years following the dissolution of my parents' marriage, and I knew what it felt like to move to a school where I felt like an outsider. Emma was disliked by several of the teachers because she was outspoken and had a hot temper, but I found her to be a sensitive writer, and in my class she was typically genial and cooperative. That is, until I gave an assignment in which the students were to critically assess a website of their own choosing.

I designed the assignment based on my perception of the students' interest in being online. I believed it would be an opportunity for students to learn how to critically read online texts and to write analytically. I thought I would be drawing on their world and building on their existing knowledge. However, Emma refused to do the assignment. She said she disliked the Internet because it made people lazy and kept them isolated. She told me she would not do the assignment because she did not want to waste her time looking at an Internet site.

Because Emma and I had established a friendly relationship, and because I respected Emma's questioning nature, I listened to her critique of the assignment. She and I negotiated a substitute assignment in which she was to write an overall critique of the Internet. As I continued working with Emma, I discovered that her discomfort had more to do with unfamiliarity with computers and lack of access to the Internet. Disliking the Internet was a defensive posture.

I also began to see that although Emma was unique in her willingness to voice an objection to an assignment, she was not unique in her discomfort with the use of computers. Other students also struggled with my assignments that depended heavily on the technology. They not only had to learn writing skills, they also had to learn computer skills—a dual task that tended to cause cognitive overload. They responded by not doing the work.

Then there were students for whom the school technology matched or was behind what they could do at home. These technologically astute students quickly completed the assigned work while secretly and not-so-secretly multitasking, so that their time on the computers included other more interesting and meaningful (to them) activities. Some students played online games. Other students busily composed lengthy e-mails and posted messages on each other's AOL home pages or Geocities websites.

About the same time, students were discovering chat rooms and instant messaging, and they figured out how to access those communication devices on the school computers even though the sites were blocked. If cell phones and texting had been as ubiquitous then as they are now, I'm sure I would have been fighting that battle as well. In the end, though, it was clear that the technologically savvy students managed to figure out how to play and do schoolwork at the same time.

As a teacher, I tried to help all of the students strengthen their writing skills. I wanted them to do well on the mandated tests and in their coursework. I also was committed to helping them learn how to use written language as a tool for making positive changes in their lives and in the world. I was frustrated by the disparity I saw among my students, and I was discouraged by the daily battles I had to fight. Furthermore, as the year went on I found that the students were not only struggling with the technology or subverting the technology to their own aims, they were also resisting my attempts to use their online activities as part of my teaching. They made it very clear that I had no business trying to appropriate their world of online fun.

In the face of these instructional setbacks, I began asking the students questions in an attempt to understand what they were doing and why they resisted my efforts. I grew even more puzzled; the students told me they hated to read, they hated to write, and that in general they hated school. Yet, I saw them reading and writing as they e-mailed their friends, created online characters, or negotiated for land, weapons, and other virtual goods that allowed them to win battles and increase their online status in games they were playing. These students, who groaned when I asked them to work together for peer revision, would willingly share hints, make suggestions, and advise each other about how best to respond to different online situations. The students told me they spent hours conversing online using message boards, e-mail, chat rooms, and instant messaging—yet they loathed spending fifteen minutes writing an essay or researching a topic assigned to them in class.

The disjunction between what students were doing on their own and what they did within the classroom began to raise questions concerning the tensions between home and in-school literacies and the way my students and I defined reading and writing. I was well aware of Heath's (1982, 1983) groundbreaking work on the mismatch between in-school and out-of-school language and literacy practices, but the presence of computer technology raised additional questions about the role of computers, online literacies, and what students were and were not doing with language. I became concerned that my attempts to build on what I perceived to be the digital knowledge of my students served to reward some and alienate others.

I also became aware that I really had little understanding of what online literacies my students were or were not engaged in and what the implications of those literacies were for their development as writers. Ultimately, I wanted to learn just what the online literacy practices of young people are, whether participation in those practices makes a difference in their lives, and if it does, what that difference is and why it matters.

This book represents something of where I am in my exploration of those questions. I have spent the past decade reading literacy theory, reading the research literature, observing youth, interviewing youth, analyzing data, mulling over the implications of what youth are doing, and trying out ways to integrate what are now being called twenty-first-century literacies into writing instruction. During those years, I have discovered that developing an approach to writing instruction for youth who have grown up in a digital world is a continual challenge.

I have found some answers to my original set of questions, but new questions arise as new technologies arise and I encounter new groups of students.

The digital world now inhabited by youth is very different from the one I first encountered in the mid-1990s. During my years of research, youth use of online tools and literacies has continued to grow and change. When I started, students were engaged in instant messaging, surfing the Web, building Web pages, sending e-mail, and playing online games. Those applications are still in use, but their popularity has faded and shifted.

Youth attention is now on texting via cell phones, engaging in social networking sites, downloading songs (legally and illegally), maintaining blogs and online journals, shopping online, watching movies online, making and posting videos, and playing online games as an avatar within a virtual world populated by a multitude of people. We are now in the world of Web 2.0, where youth are able to be active participants in creating online content. Thus, even if they do not realize it, the importance of writing or composition has gained new relevance.

In this book, I share some of what I have learned, and I have attempted to frame it in a way that teachers can apply it to their daily practice. I do not offer any easy answers, lesson plans, or reproducibles. Instead, I offer ideas to think about and to use as a jumping-off point for designing lessons that best meet the needs of your students at your school. I also attempt to address some of the concerns I often hear from teachers when discussing language, literacy, and technology. My hope is that teachers will take what I offer, adapt it, and make it their own.

Introduction

When preservice or in-service teachers talk about the role of technology in students' lives, invariably several concerns arise. First, teachers are concerned that students' heavy use of technology is hurting their ability to write well. Even teachers who are interested in using technology in their classroom and who are heavy users of digital tools themselves worry about how the different digital tools are affecting student writing skills. They point to the use of initialisms (LOL) and abbreviations (cuz) in student writing as evidence of the declining ability of students to write. They perceive that young people have more spelling errors in their writing than previous generations, and they also talk about the lack of capitalization in student writing.

Teachers are also concerned about the informal tone that young people use in their writing, as well as student resistance to writing anything longer than a short message. Despite assurances that research indicates that all those issues are really nonissues and that in fact youth are writing more than ever before, teachers remain at a loss for how to address these concerns in their classrooms.

This book is an effort to address teachers' concerns about the impact of the digital world on student writing and to suggest ways for teachers to approach these issues within a twenty-first-century literacies framework. This book is not about teaching the writing process, running a writing workshop, or using specific digital tools to support writing instruction. There are many fine publications that address those aspects of writing instruction, and this book includes an annotated bibliography of helpful resources.

The content of this book is intended to help teachers understand what the twenty-first-century literacies are, what youth are doing in respect to those literacies, and to ask how we can apply this knowledge to classroom instruction. It includes some specific suggestions, but those suggestions are meant as a jumping-off point for teachers. Nothing in this book should be taken as a recipe. The reader is encouraged to think about what is offered in each chapter and adapt it to meet the needs of his or her students within his or her specific teaching situation.

The book is divided into three parts. Chapters are intentionally short so that busy teachers will be able to read a chapter in one brief session (such as a planning period) and use what they learn in their instruction. The first part explores what it means to be young in a digital era and includes descriptions of Lisa and Joaquín (both are pseudonyms) and their literacy practices. These two students are unique in their life situation and how they use digital tools, but together they provide insight into the range of activities that Generation 2.0 participates in. This part also contains a chapter that examines multitasking and how teachers can use the tendency of Generation 2.0 to multitask to their advantage.

Part II uses the research paper, a major writing assignment that most secondary school students experience, as a way to discuss how the different elements of writing instruction can draw on the attributes of Generation 2.0 and the Web 2.0 world. The part begins with a discussion of what constitutes good writing and then moves through the process of writing a research paper, starting with data collection and ending with the proofreading and editing process. The final chapter wraps up the book by discussing how teachers can use their growing understanding of Generation 2.0 and the ways of thinking brought about by the digital revolution to be prepared for the changes that are sure to continue coming.

Part III includes a literacy and technology questionnaire to help teachers get to know their students' technology and literacy practices. An annotated list of recommended readings is provided for readers who are interested in additional suggestions for teaching writing in the digital world or who wish to know more about Generation 2.0.

Part I

UNDERSTANDING THE WORLD OF GENERATION 2.0

Chapter One

Who Is Generation 2.0?

Social forces and history shape our vision of who we are and who others are. In the United States, names have been applied to different generations as a way to identify the unique experiences and characteristics of those groups. Although the lines of demarcation are contested, there remains a general sense that there are shared traits among people born within rough sets of years. These traits were developed by the historical events and technological advances of each group's formative years and young adulthood.

For instance, the "Greatest Generation" is made up of those who were children during the Depression and fought in World War II as young adults. They are characterized by their sense of duty, work ethic, and the sacrifices they made. The "Boomer Generation," who were born after World War II and grew up in relative prosperity, are known for their sheer numbers and their rejection of the traditional values held by their parents' generation. Following the boomers came "Generation X," who grew up in the era of mass media. This generation is characterized by their pragmatism and lowered expectations for success when compared to the baby boomers. The "Millenial Generation" followed Generation X, and at the printing of this book are now young adults. They are sometimes called "digital natives," "generation next," "generation text," or the "igeneration." The millenials are said to be those who were born between 1977 and 1997.

At the writing of this book, the youngest of the millenials are entering their teens. Scholars and journalists who write about the millenials characterize them as being the first generation to have grown up in a fully digital world. They are said to differ from previous generations not only in their proclivity for using digital gadgets but also in the way they think about and approach the world. They are supposedly tribal or highly collaborative. We are told that

3

they are comfortable multitasking and uncomfortable focusing on a single task for any length of time. The characteristics of the millenials shape much of the current thinking about how to think about the digital world and its relationship to formal learning.

Now it is time to be thinking about the set of youth born after 1997 who are just entering adolescence as this book is written. This is "Generation 2.0," and we are beginning to understand that members of this newest generation expect to engage in the new literacies in ways that older members of society cannot even begin to imagine.

A large-scale survey supported by the Kaiser Family Foundation (Roberts, Foehr, & Rideout, 2008) found that eight- to eighteen-year-olds are more heavily engaged in media use than even the millenials. By virtue of multitasking, on average youth are immersed in media 7.38 hours per day, seven days a week. This includes watching television, listening to music, playing video games, using the computer, and watching movies. Children in this age group are also heavy users of mobile technology such as cell phones, which they use heavily for texting and playing video games, and iPods and MP3 players for video and music consumption. YouTube and streaming video are also used for viewing television programming. Rather than watching programs when originally broadcast, Generation 2.0 expects to watch programs at their convenience on a variety of devices. The only thing Generation 2.0 does less than the millenials is engage with print media.

Other research, such as that of literacy scholar Karen Wohlwend of Indiana University, psychologist Larry Rosen of California State University (Dominguez Hills), and cultural anthropologist Mizuko Ito of the University of California Humanities Research Institute, contributes to our growing understanding of Generation 2.0. Based on interviews with the parents of more than two thousand young children, Rosen (2010) found that children are engaging with technology at younger ages than ever before. He argues that younger children are able to multitask more items than their older siblings and have an even greater expectation of continual connectedness.

Wohlwend (2009) found that even when digital hardware and software are not available, children integrate technology into their play by creating cell phones and video games with paper and pencils or crayons. These playful activities reveal that digital technologies are an everyday part of a child's life. Ito (2008) found that young children playing in virtual worlds such as Club Penguin are learning to actively engage in their play world rather than being content to be entertained. In other words, the younger the child, the less likely he or she is to simply watch something like a television program and the more likely to expect to be able to interact with the programming at some level.

These findings may be frightening to those of us who have a strong belief in the power of traditional texts such as books, stories, and essays as tools for thinking and sharing ideas. However, the heavy use of media also carries with it the promise of engagement. Youth can be only consumers of media, but the Web 2.0 world allows for and even encourages participation. For example, the children of Generation 2.0 have grown up knowing about Webkinz, even if they did not have any. They expect to be able to use and manipulate digital materials and that digital tools are ways through which they can participate in and contribute to their world.

Members of Generation 2.0 not only watch a television program, they go online and post comments about that program, knowing that if enough people post comments about the same thing, the producers of the program listen. They not only watch videos, but if they have access to a digital video camera and editing software, they can also create and post videos. Some youth know not only how to use tools but also how to adapt the tools to their own needs or even how to create their own tools.

QUALITIES OF GENERATION 2.0

John Palfrey and Urs Gasser (2008), both legal scholars, identify a number of basic characteristics of what they refer to as the digital natives who constitute Generation 2.0.

Identity

- No separation between online identity and offline identity. A single identity is represented in different ways across multiple spaces.
- Representations of identity can be easily adjusted, but past representations can persist over time and across space.
- A digital dossier is created by the individual and by others over an individual's life and follows an individual. The construction of this dossier is out of an individual's control.

Relationship to Others

- No separation between life online and offline.
- Continually connected.
- Collaborative.
- Friendships may be short-lived but also can endure across space and time.
- Notions of privacy include the use of self-disclosure to build trust with others.

Relationship to Information

- Information is shared across time and space.
- Information is malleable.
- Information is easily accessible, and the Internet is the preferred site from which to gather information.
- Information is re-represented by reworking media using off-the-shelf software/hardware.

While the identification of these qualities is useful for thinking about ways to teach youth, we must always keep in mind that these are generalizations and may not hold true for individuals. Specifically, not all youth have the capability to be participants in the online world in the same ways. For instance, Generation 2.0, like their older siblings the millenials, have limited knowledge of the capabilities of the digital world. They engage in only those aspects that meet their immediate social needs.

Generation 2.0 may be astute users of social networking sites and avid viewers of YouTube but have little knowledge of or desire to know about digital video production. Or they may be heavily involved in video production, but know nothing of the world of fanfiction. They live in a world in which they share their activities and thoughts on an almost continuous basis through social networking, yet they have been taught to be profoundly suspicious and wary of online predators, cyberbullying, viruses, and the unknown. As such, members of Generation 2.0 may be simultaneously knowledgeable and enthusiastic, naïve and wary about different technological tools. If they are familiar with a tool, they may be almost cavalier in their use of it. If it is new, they approach it with caution.

What is important to remember is that the rapidly changing world of technology is defining Generation 2.0. Therefore, it is important to understand something about the technologies that have arisen since the birth of this newest generation.

WHAT MAKES UP THE WORLD OF GENERATION 2.0?

The first decade of the twenty-first century saw the emergence of collaborative workspaces such as wikis, social networking sites (MySpace, Facebook, LinkedIn, Webkinz, Club Penguin), virtual worlds (Second Life), widespread online gaming (World of Warcraft), social bookmarking (del.icio.us), tagging and tag clouds, podcasting, social posting of photos (Flickr), social posting of videos (YouTube), Really Simple Syndication (RSS feeds), Open ID (a single identifier and password for multiple sites), microblogging (Twitter), online video chats (Skype), and the ability to easily store and access data in "the cloud" or in file servers scattered across the Internet.

In the world of hardware, the twenty-first century has seen the arrival of smartphones that act as small computers (Blackberries, iPhones) and the near ubiquity of ordinary cell phones that are capable only of sending texts, taking video and photographs, recording voices, keeping a calendar, and so on. Additionally, we have seen an explosion in media players such as iPods and other MP3 players, electronic book readers (the Kindle, the Nook), portable video players, large-scale and portable gaming devices, touchscreens, netbooks, laptops, and tablet computing. This hardware is supported by a world connected via wireless Internet connections and mobile networks (such as the 3G network).

It is clear that we are in a period of rapid change. The technologies described allow the person with little computing expertise the ability to be continuously connected and to share and exchange ideas and information across time and space using a wide variety of modalities. Just as the printing press made the written word more accessible to the common person and ultimately brought about the Reformation, so too might the digital technologies bring about a whole new way of interacting with information, knowledge, the world, and one another.

The emergence of the technologies described above is what makes members of Generation 2.0 different from their older siblings, the millenials. Although the childhood world of the millenials was filled with media and digital technology, the technology they knew was top-down. In their Web 1.0 world, content was created by industry, institutions, and organizations. Only a few elite people with either the money or the training were able to contribute to the Internet. Interactivity via the Internet was limited to basic communications such as e-mail, chat rooms, listservs, and instant messaging. More technologically savvy users also participated in online gaming. Despite the seeming interactivity, the primary marker of the Web 1.0 world was that businesses or small groups of people created online content.

The Web 2.0 world, however, is a collective creation, and collective intelligence is a hallmark of Generation 2.0. Whereas the millenials grew up expecting to be able to use digital technologies, Generation 2.0 expects to contribute to and participate in communities created online as well as in physical space. Wikipedia is the most commonly used example of collectivity. The content of Wikipedia is created by the contributions of its members. Contributions can be large, as in the creation of an entry, or small, such as the correction of a comma placement. Despite the mistrust that many people express toward Wikipedia because it is created by the collective mind rather than by a set of established and recognized authorities, it has become one of the first sites many people visit when seeking basic information about a topic.

The idea of collectivity has extended to the communicative functions of the Internet as well. In the Web 2.0 world, communication is part of a large set of applications available to both the casual and power user. Members of Generation 2.0 no longer depend on e-mail for contacting people. Instead, an individual or groups can use social networking sites (MySpace, Facebook, Club Penguin), share ideas through videos on YouTube, post photos on Flickr, and explore ideas on blogs (initially called weblogs), microblogs, and wikis. They can also play, learn, and work in virtual worlds (such as Second Life) that they can contribute to by building not only their avatar but also the features of the world. Smartphones and wireless connections now allow people to engage in many of these activities without even needing a computer.

Furthermore, new applications, such as Twitter and Tumblr, are constantly appearing. Some are short-lived and some become part of everyday life. How long each application is popular and how people use it is unpredictable. The only thing that can be safely said is that what is here today may not be here in a few years, and what will be popular in a few years may not even have been conceived of yet.

THE DIGITAL DIVIDE/THE PARTICIPATION GAP

With such an explosion of digital tools, it is tempting to imagine and romanticize all the inventive ways for people to act as producers. However, a more realistic stance should lead us to ask who is doing what and what it means to use one tool or another.

During the mid- to late 1990s, the concept of the digital divide arose as a primary concern of policymakers and educators. The digital divide was conceived as the lack of access to hardware and software by people in impoverished communities. This included urban centers and rural areas. Schools and communities responded to this issue by getting schools connected to the Internet through broadband connections, bringing broadband into communities, and adding computers to schools, community centers, and libraries.

Most communities now have some kind of access to the Internet, although the quality of that access varies according to the socioeconomics of the area. Wealthy communities tend to have wireless access in multiple spots and easy access to state-of-the-art computers in the schools, and youth often have computers of their own. Even if they are connected to the Internet, impoverished communities, both rural and urban, tend to have slower, out-of-date computers, fewer computers, and youth may or may not have their own computers. Those youth who do have computers may have to depend on dial-up access (particularly in rural areas), which is considerably slower and less reliable than broadband.

Even though the digital divide appears to have lessened (at least according to the numbers that indicate Internet penetration), there now exists what Henry Jenkins calls the participation gap. The participation gap refers to whether people are simply consumers of Internet content or whether they contribute actively to the creation of online content. A consumer is someone who goes online to surf Web pages, read the news, or gather information about items of interest. Consumers might also play online games such as Scrabble, Bejeweled, or other digitized versions of familiar paper-and-plastic games. They might watch YouTube videos, but they do not comment on them or create their own.

Participants, in comparison, are content creators. They might play games, but when they play games they create avatars or tools and buildings in the virtual world in which they are playing. They might be writing blogs that other people read and comment on. They might read blogs but comment on those blogs, and in turn share in conversations about those ideas. They might read news articles online and share those articles through their blogs or microblogs (such as Twitter). They might watch YouTube videos, but they also respond to them by writing comments or maybe even creating their own videos in response. The possibilities for ways to engage with other people online are numerous, but the important thing to remember is that content creators become part of a community in which they share ideas. Content consumers remain on the periphery.

Henry Jenkins and his colleagues (Jenkins, Clinton, Purushotma, Robinson, & Weigel, 2006) argue that whether one is a content consumer or a content producer is important because content producers or participants learn particular skills that are valued by today's fast-paced, information-based society. These skills include the ability to

- Experiment as a way to solve problems
- Learn from simulations
- Collaborate
- Draw on multiple tools to develop knowledge
- Know how to judge various sources of information
- Adjust one's way of interacting based on the community in which one is operating
- Follow a narrative across multiple modalities such as video, a game, and status posts
- Perform different roles or identities based on the requirements of the context
- Draw from a variety of sources to create something new
- Multitask
- Search for, synthesize, and disseminate information

The fear is that people who are limited to the role of consumer do not have the opportunities to learn these skills and thus are at risk for being shut out of the economic system.

TEACHING AND THE TWENTY-FIRST-CENTURY LITERACIES

The participatory skills discussed here are similar to the twenty-first-century literacies identified by the National Council of Teachers of English (NCTE) in 2009. Before we look more closely at the idea of twenty-first-century literacies, however, we need to step back and think about what literacy and literacies are in general.

What Is Literacy?

As discussed earlier in this chapter, Generation 2.0 has different needs than those who came before, based on changes brought about by the emergence of digital technologies and a global, information-based world. Accompanying the changing needs are changing definitions of what constitutes literacy. For a very long time, the term *literacy* was rarely used or used only in the negative to indicate those who did not know how to read (*illiteracy*). Reading was seen as a cognitive and psychological act that resided within the individual. According to this view, once a person learned how to read basic school-based texts, he or she was thought to be literate.

This viewpoint is still prominent in much of educational policy. The ability to write essays has also become part of what is traditionally seen as being literate. Originally, the focus of writing instruction was handwriting or penmanship, which progressed to focus on classical rhetoric and composition. In the 1970s, with the advent of the focus on the writing process, more attention was given to students as authors. Even today, however, writing in schools often is relegated to being a form of assessment rather than being something people do to engage with ideas or to share ideas.

In the 1980s, however, our ideas of literacy began to expand. The first shift was seeing literacy as social. What that means is that we use texts within social groups for meaningful purposes, and it is those social groups that determine how a text is used and what it means. Because text use is embedded in the social world, what counts as literate changes according to the circumstances in which the text is used. In this view, being literate is not restricted to being able to read school-based texts and write school-based essays.

A person can have a rich set of literacies outside of school but still struggle in school. We can see this with youth who send text messages; create MySpace or Facebook pages; compose Web pages; write fanfiction, poetry, or rap lyrics; produce and post videos online; read graphic novels; play video games that include multiple types of texts; or make flyers to post promoting their business or band—and yet struggle to be successful in school. These are youth who by traditional measures might be considered struggling readers and writers, nonliterate, aliterate, or even illiterate, but in reality they are able to use the written word in their everyday life with ease.

In addition to seeing literacy as a social act, what is considered as text is changing because of the emergence of digital technologies. Digital technologies now allow people to create forms that include and merge video, audio, hyperlinks, and so forth. These forms are considered literate forms, but it is recognized that the forms are different from one another. Therefore, we are moving to the plural term *literacies* rather than the singular *literacy*.

What Are Twenty-First-Century Literacies?

Now that we have a sense of what literacy and literacies are, it is worthwhile to consider the definition of twenty-first-century literacies. Textbox 1.1 contains the National Council of Teachers of English (NCTE) definition.

TEXTBOX 1.1.
NCTE Definition of Twenty-first-century Literacies

Literacy has always been a collection of cultural and communicative practices shared among members of particular groups. As society and technology change, so does literacy. Because technology has increased the intensity and complexity of literate environments, the twenty-first century demands that a literate person possess a wide range of abilities and competencies, many literacies. These literacies—from reading online newspapers to participating in virtual classrooms—are multiple, dynamic, and malleable. As in the past, they are inextricably linked with particular histories, life possibilities, and social trajectories of individuals and groups. Twenty-first-century readers and writers need to

- Develop proficiency with the tools of technology
- Build relationships with others to pose and solve problems collaboratively and cross-culturally
- Design and share information for global communities to meet a variety of purposes
- Manage, analyze, and synthesize multiple streams of simultaneous information
- Create, critique, analyze, and evaluate multi-media texts
- Attend to the ethical responsibilities required by these complex environments

The NCTE definition makes clear that the idea of literacy has moved to being understood as a set of practices and a way of thinking and that literacy is also about collaboration, relationships, information collection, synthesis, and dissemination using multimedia texts. The attributes set forth by NCTE clearly parallel those described by Jenkins.

What this means, then, is that when considering technology integration, curriculum, and the needs of students and society, teachers need to move beyond thinking about what technology or tool to use. Educators should be thinking instead about what kind of thinking they want to engage students in and then select the technological tool that is most appropriate for that type of engagement.

Approaching the issue of literacy instruction for Generation 2.0 through the lens of twenty-first-century literacies as opposed to that of technology integration also avoids the problem of out-of-date technologies in the classroom, the need to chase down the most up-to-date software or hardware, or teacher unfamiliarity with a particular piece of software or hardware. By approaching instruction through a twenty-first-century literacies lens rather than a technology integration lens, we shift the focus from the technology to the ways of thinking supported by participatory tools, and the ways of thinking have a much longer shelf life than do the transitory technologies that make up the Web 2.0 world.

THE ROLE OF TECHNOLOGY

Despite the need to take the focus off technology, we should not ignore technology, either. Obviously, the definition of twenty-first-century literacies is tightly tied to the presence of technology. What is interesting to consider, however, is that technology has always been connected to literacy. Dennis Baron (2001), in his article "From Pencils to Pixels," describes the relationship of technology to literacy through a discussion of the development of the pencil. Today most people would not consider a pencil to be a piece of technology. Technology now is typically associated with those things that are digital.

However, as Baron points out, marking symbols on a clay tablet with a stylus or scratching letters on paper with a wood-encased piece of graphite both involve the use of human-made artifacts—that is, technology. Furthermore, the stylus and the clay tablet, the pencil and the paper, or the keyboard connected to the Internet change our relationship to the written word and to each other. What happens is that once a technology works smoothly and is an integral part of life, we forget that it is a technology. So now when we think of technology, we think only of that which is new to us, that which we are not yet comfortable with, or that which breaks down frequently and in doing so raises our awareness that it is a technology. Thus, we tend to forget that the landline telephone is technology, but we remember that the cell phone is—or at least whenever it drops a call or we get a new phone with new functions to learn.

Our understanding of what constitutes technology is important because what we consider technology may differ from what our students consider technology. What we consider new and mysterious and maybe even a little frightening may be just another tool that students use as part of their repertoire of communicative practices. Or we might assume that all youth are engaged in something because it is digitally based, but it might be new and intimidating to our students because they have not yet encountered it as part of their social life.

Ultimately, we need to think about what social practices we want our youth to engage in and then consider what tools are available to accomplish those goals. Therefore, there may be times when paper-and-pen technology is the appropriate tool and other times when cutting-edge digital products will best meet our needs. The key, as in all good teaching practice, starts with our learning goals and objectives.

LEARNING IN THE TWENTY-FIRST CENTURY

Thus far we've defined Generation 2.0, literacy, and technology. We now turn to a discussion of why this all matters in light of learning in the twenty-first century.

The changes to the world brought about by the digital technologies and the emerging globalized information economy require a different kind of learning than that experienced by people who grew up in the twentieth century. Participatory culture, or a way of using text that moves a person from being a consumer of texts to a producer of content, supports and is supported by a collaborative approach to the world. This collaborative approach to the world, therefore, requires a rethinking of how people learn and what teaching should look like.

In many ways, twenty-first-century learning is a return to the original agrarian or community-based learning that occurred before industrialization. Prior to industrialization, a child learned how to be a member of the community by working alongside accomplished elders. This elder may have been a parent, grandparent, accomplished neighbor or craftsperson, or even an older sibling or cousin. By first observing and then taking up tasks alongside the elder, whether in the shop or in the field, the child slowly became more accomplished at the tasks required to maintain the health of the community. When the child was unable to accomplish something on his or her own, the elder was there to guide and assist as needed. As the child grew more accomplished, the elder withdrew support accordingly.

This style of teaching and learning is what Rogoff (1990, 2003) calls an apprenticeship model. Rogoff documented this type of learning among the indigenous populations of Mexico, but most people can recall experiencing this type of learning in their own life. It may have been how you learned to cook, repair a small engine, or do home renovations. Rather than being tested on a discrete set of skills, such as hammering a nail, you knew you had learned how to do something when you were able to do it on your own. Ultimately, learning is marked by how your participation in your community changes. The more you learn, the more you are able to participate and be an active member of your community.

All this may sound familiar to educators. It is what Lev Vygotsky (1978) called the zone of proximal development. Specifically, the zone of proximal development is the point where the learner is not quite able to do something on his or her own but can do it with the assistance of someone more expert in the task. By working with an expert, the learner is able to achieve more than he or she would be able to on his or her own.

Most formal education as it occurs in schools has moved away from the apprenticeship model of learning. Schools were set up based on developmental models of learning, in which a child was believed to be ready for certain tasks based on age. Furthermore, in order to protect children from being exploited as factory labor, they were moved out of the flow of the community and into the classroom. Although much was gained through this model, we lost sight of what people learn within a community and children lost a connection to the community. With the advent of the twenty-first-century literacies and participatory culture, we now have the need to reacquaint ourselves with this understanding of learning. Accompanying this shift is the opportunity to reconnect youth with the larger community, which may in turn address some of the alienation that youth have experienced since the advent of industrialized society.

One of the exciting aspects of participatory culture, however, is that it expands the apprenticeship model beyond the expert/learner model. The Web 2.0 world allows for tasks to be accomplished collaboratively, with each person contributing at the level he or she is able to and each contribution being equally important to the community. Bruns (2008) calls this equipotentiality. The idea of equipotentiality recognizes that no one person in the community holds all the expertise, but everyone in the community is capable of contributing to the task at hand. It is the collaborative mind or the collective intelligence of all members of the community working in concert that supports the completion of a socially meaningful task. This collective intelligence is made possible through the use of digital tools that let us transcend space and time.

The general idea, then, is that learning in a Web 2.0 world or participatory culture is built on an ethos of collaboration and community. Youth expect to be constantly connected in some way, and this constant connection is used to be part of a group and to build the knowledge that is important to that group. A task for teachers is to integrate the ethos of participatory culture into the classroom so that all students can benefit. This includes helping students who are on the consumer side of the participation gap acquire the participatory skills required for membership in today's information-based society.

SUMMARY

Generation 2.0 is the group of people who were born after 1997 and have grown up not only in a digital world but in a world in which they expect to be participants and contribute to the creation of their online experience. They are immersed in digital media and have always known that digital tools are available to keep them constantly connected. Members of Generation 2.0 share a set of characteristics that include how they use digital tools to construct their identity, manage their privacy, connect to their friends, and collaboratively work with and understand information. However, not all people who are in Generation 2.0 have the same access to the digital world. A participation gap exists between those youth who are members of a participatory culture in which they actively use the tools of Web 2.0 and those youth who are on the fringes and simply use or consume the products created by others.

Generation 2.0 came about as a part of the emergence of the Web 2.0 world. Web 2.0 includes a wide constellation of ever-evolving digital tools that allow for easy participation in the online world. Through participation in the Web 2.0 world, youth learn a set of skills that range from the willingness to experiment to solve problems, to using simulations, collaborating, moving through different communities, performing different roles, multitasking, and finding, using, and disseminating information across different modalities.

Educational organizations such as NCTE have defined the twenty-first-century literacies to include the understanding that literacy is a social act, done for a purpose within a community. This is consistent with the body of literacy research conducted since the 1980s. The idea of twenty-first-century literacies adds in the idea that multimedia texts are part of the repertoire of literacy practices people use. The twenty-first-century literacies are also called the new literacies.

Given the changing nature of youth, literacy, and technology, teachers who wish to integrate the new literacies into their teaching need to consider the type of thinking supported by the new literacies rather than focusing on the technology. Teachers also need to recognize that learning in the Web 2.0 world is akin to the apprenticeship model of the past but supported by the theories of Vygotsky. By reconsidering our understanding of learning and thinking, we are able to identify what it is we want to occur during a learning experience and then pick the best technology for the experience, rather than just adding a convenient piece of technology to an existing learning task.

Chapter Two

What We Can Learn
from Lisa and Joaquín

The two very different students described in this chapter are members of the Millenial Generation, not Generation 2.0, but their experiences with digital technology provide insights into the world of Generation 2.0. It is important to remember that each young person is unique in his or her life situation and in how he or she uses digital technology. Thus readers will most likely find that any digital youth they know will be similar to Lisa and Joaquín in some ways and very different in others. The purpose of sharing their stories is so that readers can see how these two young people use the wide range of digital tools that are available to them and what those tools mean to each of them. With this framework in mind, teachers can then begin to see the students they work with in a new light.

LISA

Lisa is a European-American female who attended a magnet high school in a mid-size city in western New York State. Like many of her friends, she preferred to dress in casual clothes such as jeans, T-shirts, and sneakers. Her magnet school focused on arts education, and Lisa was a creative writing major. She considered herself to be a leader and often took on the role of organizing activities for her group of friends, which consisted of a core group of five young men and women with whom she had been friends since elementary school and junior high. Lisa maintained her friendships through high school, college, and into early adulthood.

When she was young, Lisa was diagnosed with an auditory processing disability and received instructional modifications that included being spelling exempt, using a scribe or word processor, and being allowed additional time on tests. In high school, she was a high-achieving student and took numerous honors and advanced placement courses as well as a range of electives; she graduated second in her class. After graduation from high school, she attended an elite private college, where she majored in economics.

When Lisa was fifteen, she characterized herself as a "hardcore user" of instant messaging. At that time she was on the computer for sixteen to twenty hours a week, and of that time eleven to fifteen hours were spent engaged in instant messaging. She also e-mailed a bit, surfed online, and did some online shopping. At the time she did not have a cell phone, although there was a landline telephone next to the computer she used in the family den. She also used the computer for writing essays, short stories, and poems for school.

By the time she was seventeen, Lisa used instant messaging far less than she had when younger because she was seldom home in the afternoon. Her after-school time was spent either on sports such as soccer or ultimate disc, taking guitar and clarinet lessons, participating in the school's debate team, or taking a Scholastic Achievement Test preparatory course. Instead of using instant messaging to converse with distant friends, she used away status messages (Facebook was not yet common) to alert her friends as to her whereabouts. She occasionally used instant messaging when she was studying as a way to get an answer to a question regarding the homework or to reassure herself that her friends were working just as hard as she on school assignments.

Contrary to popular belief that instant messaging damages youths' ability to write, Lisa developed strong writing skills. In fact, she won awards for her creative writing efforts, including a national award for a haiku and the honor of having her one-act play staged at the local regional theater.

Table 2.1 shows the literacies Lisa engaged in on a regular basis during her last three years of high school. The list is divided into those activities she did on her own for fun and those she did for school.

Table 2.1. Lisa's Literacies

Leisure	School
Instant messaging	Reading novels
E-mail	Reading textbooks
Internet shopping	Reading news articles
Reading news articles	Writing essays
	Writing plays
	Writing poetry
	Writing short stories
	E-mail
	Instant messaging

From the list, we can see that the majority of Lisa's reading and writing activities originated in school. In fact, even though Lisa said she liked to read for pleasure, she did not because her heavy workload from school did not allow her the time to do so. It is also notable that Lisa's school-based literacies were traditional and nondigital except for the use of a computer for word processing. There is also some crossover with the digital tools, in that instant messaging and e-mail were often used to support her completion of school assignments. These digital tools, however, were not assigned tasks as were the reading of texts and writing of specific genres such as plays, poetry, essays, and short stories. The digital tools were used to support the traditional school assignments.

Lisa's development as a strong writer came about through the support of her parents as well as her schooling. Because both her parents were professionals, her home was filled with texts related to their jobs. Her family was also politically and socially active, and they consistently engaged in conversations about politics and social issues. Her choice to major in creative writing at an arts magnet high school allowed her to explore a wide variety of genres as a writer and to share her writing with a community of professional writers. Teachers in her school were published authors, and students were routinely encouraged to enter their writing in regional and national competitions.

Her development was not without its challenges, however. When Lisa was young, she was diagnosed with a language processing disability. This label allowed her extended time on tests, the use of a word processor for essay writing, and exemption from being penalized for poor spelling. As a result of this, Lisa saw herself as a bad speller. She said her friends recognized that her messages to them would be full of spelling mistakes.

Despite Lisa's supposed disability, her writing for school was error free, and she consistently corrected her spelling as she was writing instant messages. Granted, she did not correct all her mistakes, but she did when there was a risk that the person on the other side of the conversation might misunderstand. Moreover, Lisa seldom used the abbreviations associated with instant messaging (such as LOL for "laughing out loud"). Most words were spelled out. She also paid closer attention to her instant messages when she was engaged in a serious conversation with a friend than when she was joking around and just passing time. In other words, serious online conversations were longer and had fewer errors in them. The use of Internet language and misspellings only occurred when Lisa was engaged in spontaneous writing during instant messaging—an act similar to a casual conversation.

In sum, Lisa was engaged as a writer at multiple levels that connected her to a variety of communities. She was connected to her school community through the essay she wrote for class. It was to Lisa's advantage to stay connected to the school culture because one of her goals was to do well in school so that she could attend an elite college. Lisa was connected to the larger artistic community of her city through her participation in writing competitions.

The connections Lisa built helped her achieve her goal of college admission. Her literacies also contributed to strong family relationships. Both her parents were heavy users of text as part of their jobs and as part of their engagement in social issues. By reading news articles, she was able to participate in conversations around the dinner table and in social gatherings hosted by her parents. Finally, her use of instant messaging kept her connected to her friends. This supported her social and emotional needs and allowed her to grow into a healthy and independent adult.

JOAQUÍN

Joaquín is an eighteen-year-old Latino male in the same urban school district as Lisa. He emigrated to the United States from the Dominican Republic when he was sixteen. His first language is Spanish, he studied French when he lived in the Dominican Republic, and he spoke casual English fluently and struggled with writing academic English. To address his English language learning needs, Joaquín attended a large comprehensive high school that offered bilingual support.

After moving to the United States, Joaquín first lived with his brother in New York City and then joined his father and stepmother in western New York. He said he moved to the United States because he saw that his brother was able to help his mother and grandmother financially, and he wanted to be able to do the same. He said he left New York City because after visiting his father and stepmother, he decided he liked the opportunity the schools in the smaller city offered and he was able to find a part-time job at a fast food restaurant. He said he wanted to use the money from his job to help his father, who has diabetes, as well as send some to his mother and grandmother, but his parents insisted he save the money for college. He disagreed with his parents and was planning on finding a second job so that he could use one check to contribute to his family's finances and save the other check.

Joaquín planned to move back to New York City after he graduated from high school. He hoped to eventually go to college there in order to become a mechanical engineer. He was particularly interested in New York City because of its fast pace. He said the city where he was attending high school was boring.

Before moving to the United States, Joaquín attended a private school where he learned French and was introduced to the digital technologies. His mother's boyfriend, who is a tour guide, taught him how to make videos and post the videos to YouTube. One of his first video productions was a reenactment of the uprising against Rafael Trujillo, former president and military leader of the Dominican Republic. He wrote the script and directed the movie. His cousins were the actors. At that time, he also started writing and recording his own music.

After he moved to the United States, Joaquín continued making videos, writing lyrics (in Dominican Spanish), and making beats (using prerecorded sounds to create music for dancing or rapping to). By the time he was eighteen, he had made more than ten videos on his own, some of which he posted on YouTube. He was also proud of the fact that he wrote and produced his own beats and songs. When making beats, Joaquín said he would start with existing pieces of music and then manipulate them using software in order to "make it his own." He would then layer those beats over one another to create something new. Joaquín used a variety of free software programs such as Moviemaker, Frooty Loops, and CooleditPro for his Windows-based computer at home to make his music and videos.

In order to support his music making, Joaquín built a recording studio in his home. The studio included a microphone, headphones, a computer, and an amplifier. He dreamed of building a larger studio and buying an Apple computer, which he said was better for mixing music and video. Joaquín taught himself how to use GarageBand, a popular Apple software product for creating music, even though he did not have an Apple computer. Under a stage name, Joaquín established a MySpace page and a YouTube account that he uses to promote and distribute his music. He also performed his music at the school's talent show and posted the video of his performance on YouTube. Most of his music is written and sung in Dominican Spanish, but he said he has been writing more in English in order to improve his English.

Joaquín also taught himself different poetic forms so that he could be a better rap author. He said he did not like freestyle rapping, which is improvisational, so he was learning different rhyme patterns. His content, however, was informed by his life and included thoughts about what happened to him as a child, love, violence, the war in Iraq, and people dying in the streets. He said he also wrote songs for friends to use when wooing their girlfriends. When writing his lyrics, Joaquín said he refused to use profanity because he wanted to show people how he respected the music and take care of what he represents. Joaquín also tried his hand at writing longer texts. In fact, during his senior year of high school, he read Julia Alvarez's *In the Time of Butterflies*, and inspired by the book, he started writing his own book about his country.

Joaquín was less successful in school than Lisa, and he had a different set of challenges to overcome. He had been in the United States for a little less than two years before he was expected to graduate from high school and be prepared for college. He was fluent in conversational English, but his academic language and writing in English was still developing. His academic essays tended to be very short and filled with errors in word choice and grammar, consistent with his stage in second-language acquisition.

Joaquín's development as a writer and his sense of success were based primarily on his digital literacies. For instance, he created podcasts and videos for his school that won acclaim from teachers. In a video he created for a class assignment, he created a rap video about ways to stop gang violence. Based on the research he read as part of his class, he wrote lyrics that addressed why youth join gangs and what can be done to address the problems of gangs. He said he was also asked to create a video about his school that could be shown to visitors.

As can be seen in table 2.2, Joaquín's literacies are very different from Lisa's. Whereas Lisa's literacies were primarily based in school, many of Joaquín's literate activities occurred outside of school. Thus, even though Lisa was the more successful student, it could be argued that Joaquín has the wider range of literacy practices and thus may be better equipped for negotiating the Web 2.0 world.

Table 2.2. Joaquín's Literacies

Leisure	School
Making beats	Reading novels
E-mail	Reading textbooks
Texting	Writing essays and reports
Writing lyrics	Writing and producing movies
Writing and producing movies	Writing and producing podcasts
Writing poetry	
Writing a novel	

It is also interesting to note that video production crossed between school and leisure literacy practices for Joaquín. This happened only because his teachers supported his interest in movies. If they had insisted on formal academic writing only, Joaquín most likely would have had no areas in which he could excel in school and successfully demonstrate his learning.

When he was writing for school, Joaquín's teachers focused on specific content as well as language form. All the students tended to write very short pieces, often writing in Spanish and then translating those pieces into English. When writing outside of school, such as when texting, Joaquín and his classmates would write in whichever language was most appropriate for their intended recipient. As such they were developing as biliterate writers.

Joaquín and his classmates said they did not worry about spelling errors when texting. However, when writing in Spanish on the computer, he did pay attention to diacritical marks and knew the keystrokes needed to insert the correct symbols into Spanish language writing.

Although his teacher tried to impress upon the students the importance of originality and the dangers of plagiarism, Joaquín and his classmates leaned heavily on preexisting English language sentences in order to create their essays. They would cut and paste texts from websites and then stitch the sentences together rather than create their own sentences. In many respects, this cut-and-paste form of essay writing is similar to how Joaquín mixed his beats. As he said, he would take a beat and then "make it his own." This was not seen as plagiarism but rather as a foundation for something new. The cut-and-paste approach also helped him take steps toward academic English. The challenge for Joaquín is to move beyond copying to rephrasing.

Overall, Joaquín was developing as a writer outside of school and becoming connected to a community of rappers and amateur video producers. His connection to school literacies was tenuous and existed most strongly only when teachers acknowledged and built on his knowledge of digital tools. Joaquín wanted to stay connected to the school because he saw school as a way to get ahead in life, but he was torn between that and wanting to provide immediate support to his family by working a second job. Joaquín's use of digital tools primarily connected him to his friends. Myspace, YouTube, and texting are predominantly youth oriented, and the ways in which he used those tools did not build his ability to move toward his goal of attending college for a degree in mechanical engineering. In fact, Joaquín expressly rejected the idea of using his skills in digital technologies as a jumping-off point for a career.

What is important to remember about Joaquín's story is that his use of writing and digital tools had a purpose in his life and contributed to his participation in a youth community as well as to his growing identity as a successful and literate person. Moreover, his strongest connection to school was through these literacies rather than through traditional literacies. Joaquín could be considered a youth at high risk for not succeeding in school, and it may have been his teachers' acceptance of his digital projects that helped move him toward graduation.

SUMMARY

Lisa was a successful high school student with a variety of literacy practices both in and out of school. Because her high school experience took place in a school with an arts focus and Lisa was a creative writing major, she had many opportunities to write in school. However, because of her heavy academic load, her literacy practices outside of school were fairly limited. Those literacy practices she did for fun were centered around digital tools and included instant messaging, online shopping, and reading the news so that she could have interesting conversations with her politically active parents.

Joaquín engaged in more literacy practices outside of school than Lisa and was a less successful student, mostly because he was still learning academic English. He wrote poetry and raps, mixed beats, and made songs and videos that he posted online. He also made podcasts for his school. His success in school was mostly because his teachers supported his development of digital media skills. His skill with digital tools connected him to a larger community of rap artists and friends outside of school.

These two students illustrate the different ways youth can engage in digital tools. Their experiences should not be generalized to other students. However, we can use Lisa's and Joaquín's experiences for insights into the ways different students can be supported through the use of both traditional and new literacies.

Chapter Three

Making Friends with Multitasking

One of the biggest things we know about members of Generation 2.0 is they have a heavy tendency to multitask. As noted earlier in this book, research has shown that on average youth are immersed in media 7.38 hours per day, seven days a week. This includes watching television, listening to music, playing video games, using the computer, watching movies, and using their cell phones to do these things as well as to text. These actions result in youth consuming tremendous amounts of media content, which in turn increases the risk of information overload.

Teachers and parents often wonder how youth manage to accomplish anything when they multitask and worry that the children in their care are not learning as well as they could. Rosen (2010) tells us that youth are adept at multitasking and are able to do almost anything while multitasking, even if it takes a little longer than if they had focused on one task at a time. However, other research shows that some people are better than others in multitasking. A recent study by Watson and Strayer of the University of Utah (in press) showed that of their study participants, 2.5 percent were "supertaskers." That is, they were able to multitask with minimal cognitive losses. However, most people do experience some form of cognitive loss or inattention during multitasking, even if they swear they can multitask with no problem.

INFORMATION OVERLOAD

One of the risks of multitasking is information overload. Information overload occurs when more information is coming in than a person can cognitively handle. There are five main causes of information overload. Of course, these things happen in any situation regardless of the Internet, but the Internet makes it worse and has also made the issue of multitasking more visible. Each of these causes has direct implications for teaching, which will be discussed in this chapter.

1. The development and use of information technologies. This has made more information available than ever before.
2. The organizational design of today's world. Today's business environment demands that people collaborate more. Youth too are used to collaboration. The downside of collaboration, however, is that more information comes in from multiple sources and needs to be dealt with.
3. The varying quality of information. When people need to make decisions about the quality of the information, they become overloaded.
4. The nature of the task itself. A new, complex task that requires taking in a large amount of material will cause overload. This happens even in non-digital environments. For instance, in graduate-level classes that require a great deal of reading of complex material, students often suffer overload and struggle to understand the material.
5. Insufficient skill, qualification, experience, and motivation of the reader. If the reader doesn't have the needed background knowledge or skills for making sense of a text, he or she becomes overloaded.

When information overload happens, people respond in a variety of ways.

- They spend less time with each piece of information.
- They use filtering devices to eliminate the less compelling or relevant material.
- They only respond to simple messages, requests, or questions.
- They write simpler messages as overload increases.
- They stop participating.
- They use strategies to remove distractions.

What happens is that when people start putting their overload reaction strategies into action, they are less likely to seek out a wide range of sources; they focus on those sites that already fit with what they know rather than seeking divergent information. The end result of these actions is that the student ends up with a superficial understanding of whatever issue is being explored. The student also fails to engage critically with the material.

Research in cognition tells us that multitasking does not work when a person is attempting to learn something new or trying to do something that requires a great deal of concentration. However, there are also times when multitasking is appropriate. If a person is engaged in a rote activity that requires little concentration, multitasking is a natural fit. For example, most adults commonly do household tasks such as laundry or dishwashing. Very often music may be playing, a television might be on, or the person could be talking on the telephone or to a person in the room. On the other hand, completing the federal 1040 tax form generally requires more concentration and thus a quieter and calmer environment. The trick is helping students to recognize what their cognitive needs are when engaging in a task and to make the choice that works best for them.

A look at how Lisa multitasked demonstrates how youth negotiate cognitive demands and handle information overload. For instance, in one case, she ended a telephone conversation when she had to turn her attention to a serious instant messaging conversation with a close friend. In another case, she stopped instant message exchanges with her boyfriend for a brief time in order to have a telephone conversation with a classmate about an upcoming exam.

However, when Lisa was involved in lighthearted instant message conversations, she was able to stay connected to a number of people at the same time. Lisa also was able to use multitasking to her advantage even when she was involved in a task that required concentration. One example is when she was studying for an advanced placement history exam. During a one-hour study session, she switched between a telephone conversation, several instant messaging conversations, and reading her class notes. Although it initially appeared that Lisa's focus was scattered, a closer examination of her activities revealed that the instant message conversations and the phone conversation were all related to studying. In other words, what appeared to be a case of distractedness was actually her engaging in a virtual study group using several different technologies to stay connected.

LEVERAGING MULTITASKING FOR WRITING INSTRUCTION

Given what we know about youth tendencies for multitasking, the realities of information overload, and how youth respond to information overload, what can teachers do to help students develop the wherewithal to determine when multitasking is appropriate and when it is not, and teach them how to use multitasking to their advantage in learning environments?

First, it is important to recognize that lecturing students on the importance of unitasking will not work. Having developed skill at multitasking, students will resist demands to unitask. Instead, teachers and students should engage in open, nonjudgmental conversations about the multitasking behaviors youth engage in, how to identify signs of information overload, and the various reactions people have to information overload. Teachers and students can then work together to develop strategies for responding to information overload that will not result in the loss of learning.

For instance, when planning a writing assignment, the teacher can identify the cognitive demands of the different tasks within a writing assignment and discuss with the students different strategies for finding success with those tasks. The students and teacher can work together to identify the tasks that are conducive to multitasking and those that would best be performed alone. This identification should be differentiated by student because each student comes to the writing assignment with a unique background and skill set, which we know affects information overload. Teachers should also be careful not to impose their own limitations at multitasking on students; however, if a student shows evidence of struggling with a task, the teacher should guide the student in determining whether his or her decision about multitasking was appropriate.

AN EXAMPLE: A SAMPLE WRITING ASSIGNMENT

This assignment is based on the first one given to college freshmen in a content area course titled Literacies and Justice. This course, which can be applied toward the Peace and Social Justice minor, is linked to the first-semester English composition course. The assignment is intended to begin guiding students toward thinking about their identities as readers and writers and how texts can either silence people or help them develop voice. Although this assignment was developed for first-semester college freshmen, the basic structure and planning process can be used in any grade level.

Although the Web 2.0 world is multimodal and Generation 2.0 is comfortable in a multimodal world, this essay is intentionally unimodal and depends entirely on alphabetic text and ink-and-paper technology. As stated earlier in this book, this is because the world of schooling still values and privileges the traditional essay, and if we are to do service to our students, we must help them develop skills in traditional composition forms. What should be noted, however, is that this essay assignment is actually the first step in a semester-long project that results in a multimodal group project.

Writing prompt: *In this paper, you will describe a moment in your life when literacy played an important role. You will use the course readings to understand how this moment helped you develop your identity as a literate and powerful person, or how it contributed to feelings of powerlessness and lack of success as a literate person.*

Knowing students' penchant for multitasking, we might assume a student's first response would be to put on the headphones, select songs to listen to, turn on the computer and open up the word processing program, open up Facebook, maybe open up instant messaging, and check the cell phone for text messages. The student then might read through the assignment and begin tapping out a memory of a literacy event. In between spurts of writing, he or she might change song selections, check Facebook, send a few text messages, and talk to a roommate. After writing the memory, the student might take a second look at the writing prompt and notice that it is asking for analysis based on the course readings. At this point, information overload might begin. Writing the memory was easy; figuring out what the course readings have to do with it and what it all means is not.

Based on what we know about how people respond to information overload, we can assume the filters will go up. The student will respond to the simple messages—maybe questions about lunch or weekend plans. The student might open up his or her notes, but the ping of the cell phone with a new message can be tended to more easily than figuring out how to connect the difficult course readings to something the student experienced when younger. The student taps out a short answer to the message, then turns back to the assignment and the readings. What did those readings really mean? The student flips through the notes and looks at the annotations he or she made. They are not making a lot of sense.

Our freshman might then broadcast a message to friends who are in the same class, asking if any of them understand the assignment. Answers immediately start to come in on the cell phone. The student now has to sort through the various messages and figure out which ones are helpful and which ones are not. Eventually the student gives up, feeling inadequate to the task. Later, he or she talks with a few friends in person and online, and together they come up with some ideas for the essay. That night, just a few short hours before the essay is due, the student completes the essay by pulling a few quotes out of the readings that he or she thinks have something to do with the literacy event described. The student submits the essay and hopes for a good enough grade. The student tells himself or herself that he or she never was a very good writer and it was a stupid assignment anyway.

In this scenario, we can see the five causes of information overload and the resulting behaviors described earlier in this chapter. We can also see some of the characteristic behaviors of Generation 2.0.

First, we can see that the plethora of information technologies created a constant flow of data. This constant connection allows our student to connect to others for help, but results in the need to sort through multiple sources and to determine the quality of those responses. The nature of the task also contributes to information overload. Writing the memory is easy because the student has had a great deal of experience writing personal narrative, starting in kindergarten and first grade. Analysis, however, is something fairly new. And using material from texts the student barely understands is even more challenging. He or she has neither the experience nor skills to deal with this part of the assignment.

Our student responds with several of the coping strategies identified by Palfrey and Gasser (2008). First, because the texts are difficult, the student does not spend much time working through them. Instead, the student turns to those things he or she knows how to deal with—simple messages on the cell phone. Finally, the student stops participating. What helps the student finally complete the assignment, however, is the constant connection and collaboration with friends. Through face-to-face conversations as well as text messages, the student gathers enough ideas and strategies for finishing the essay. It might not be an "A" essay, the student thinks, but at least it is finished.

LEVERAGING MULTITASKING
AND MINIMIZING INFORMATION

What then, could a teacher do to minimize some of the difficulties the described student experienced and to actually use the tendency to multitask to the student's advantage?

First, let us look at the individual tasks required to successfully complete the assignment and consider what the cognitive load is for each task. We can then consider what type of environment is needed in order to support success.

Writing prompt: *In this paper, you will describe a moment in your life when literacy played an important role. You will use the course readings to understand how this moment helped you develop your identity as a literate and powerful person, or how it contributed to feelings of powerlessness and lack of success as a literate person.*

Task 1: Identify a moment when literacy played an important role
Cognitive load: Low
Teacher plan:

   a. As a class, review several models of literacy memories to identify the qualities of the text.
   b. The teacher models the brainstorming and drafting using a personal memory.
   c. Use the collaborative nature of Generation 2.0 to brainstorm ideas and share memories. This could be done orally in class or using texting or a discussion board/moodle outside of class.

Task 2: Describe the literacy event
Cognitive load: Low to medium, depending on writing skill of the student
Teacher plan:

    a. Discuss how multitasking will interact with this task. For most students multitasking should not be detrimental. In fact, multitasking may help by permitting students to share ideas with one another, look at artifacts that represent the moment, or communicate with people who have knowledge of the memory they are describing.

    b. Have the students write the first draft of the memory as homework.

Task 3: Use course readings to understand the event
Cognitive load: Medium to high, depending on reading comprehension skills of the students and the difficulties of the texts
Teacher plan: In order to complete this portion of the assignment, students must be able to do two subactions: They must have a solid understanding of the texts. They also must have analytic skills. The first two steps are required *before giving the assignment* if students are to successfully complete the assignment.

    a. Hold class discussions to clarify the meanings of the texts.

    b. Have students write summary microthemes (see the work of John Bean for detailed information on microthemes) following the discussions. Microthemes are brief essays (often limited to one side of a 5" × 8" index card). A microtheme allows the teacher to quickly and easily assess whether the student has grasped the material and also supports student understanding of the material. A summary microtheme asks students to identify the main idea, supporting points, and connections among the parts of the text. Students must condense the content by weeding out the less important elements of the text while maintaining the hierarchy between ideas. The summary microtheme also leads the student away from imposing his or her opinion on the reading, going off topic, or misrepresenting the author's ideas.

    c. Model analysis. Use the teacher-generated text to model the descriptive portion of the assignment. Examine the description and demonstrate how the material from the course readings can be used to understand the event.

    d. Share an example of a written analysis with the students and have the students identify where and how the texts were used to analyze the event.

    e. Discuss how this is most likely a new type of assignment for the students and that multitasking will probably lead to information overload.

Therefore, urge students to work on this during short, dedicated bursts of time.

f. Provide in-class time for drafting the analysis.

- It may be helpful to use the collaborative nature of Generation 2.0 to assist in the initial analysis. Partners or small groups of students could go through each student's description and identify which readings are relevant and how they are relevant.
- Write the first section of the analysis in class. As students are writing, hold one-on-one writing conferences with the students to identify areas of strength and where support is needed, and to clear up misconceptions and areas of confusion.

g. Students write the whole draft as homework. Subsequent drafts could be workshopped in class as required.

This lesson is similar to what teachers already do in supporting writing development, but the difference is that it was designed to address what we know about the nature of Generation 2.0. It is intended to build on the collaborative nature of the students as well as to acknowledge the realities of multitasking and information overload. Although teachers may bemoan the fact that students multitask, it is to our advantage to admit to the realities of the Web 2.0 world and use them to our advantage. At the same time, it is our duty to not only help students develop the skills for creating texts in the Web 2.0 world, but also to explicitly guide them in their meta-awareness of their behaviors.

SUMMARY

Multitasking is one of the hallmarks of Generation 2.0, and it has become one of the major concerns of teachers as well as psychologists and cognitive researchers. Recent research indicates that most people cannot multitask without some loss of cognitive abilities, even though most people argue that they are effective multitaskers. Rather than fighting multitasking, teachers can use students' desire to multitask to their advantage and teach students when it is appropriate to multitask and when it is more advantageous to unitask.

One of the major problems with multitasking and the constant influx of information from the always-on digital world is cognitive overload. Cognitive overload can come from a variety of sources, including the way an organization or task is designed, the varying quality of information, and the quantity of information coming in. When people are cognitively overloaded, they filter out information, pick the simplest tasks to perform, remove distractions, or stop participating. The end result is poorer performance on a given task.

By analyzing the components within a lesson and assignment, the teacher can identify where cognitive overload might occur and design the task so that students will be able to unitask during the cognitively loaded moments and will be allowed to multitask during the less challenging parts of the assignment.

Chapter Four

What Is Good Writing?

One of the key problems facing teachers, or any reader for that matter, is determining the quality of a text. Here we approach this problem from two perspectives: that of a reader and that of a writer. First, when sorting through the plethora of material presented to us in both ink-and-paper form and now in digital form, we must decide what is worth taking the time to read, and what we should pass over. Second, when working as a writer or guiding students in their development as writers, we need to determine what constitutes good writing.

IDENTIFYING QUALITY SOURCES

Traditionally in English Arts classes, texts worth reading are identified by virtue of their place in the literary canon. In other content areas, valued texts are those that have been vetted by respected publishers (such as textbook publishers). In the world of scholarship, quality is determined through the process of blind peer review in which other experts in the field determine whether the text meets the requirements of the discipline. In each of these cases, experts determine the level of quality.

This is changing in the Web 2.0 world. In their book *Born Digital: Understanding the First Generation of Digital Natives*, Palfrey and Gasser suggest that determining quality when it comes to online material is more complicated because of the sheer quantity of information that is available. The issue is further complicated by the fact that the participatory nature of the Web 2.0 world makes it so that almost anyone can post information online without having the quality of the text checked. Teachers have been tackling this issue for a number of years, and there are numerous recommendations that have been made and lesson plans that are available for teaching students how to determine the trustworthiness of an online text.

Reading theory tells us that a person's response to a text, and whether people find a text useful or meaningful, is based on the background of the people, the prior knowledge they bring to the text, whether the text fits with what they already know or challenges what they know, and what it is they want to do with the text. This is true whether the text is ink marks on paper or in multiple modes online. However, determining the quality of multimodal texts is in some ways more complicated than determining the quality of traditional texts. Specifically, research tells us that youth judge the value of a text by page design, including color, typeface, and the complexity of design. In other words, a Web page that looks "professional" is determined to be more trustworthy than an amateurish page.

Youth are also swayed by the amount of text; text-heavy Web pages are seen as being more trustworthy. This interestingly suggests a paradox, because youth prefer Web pages that include images or graphics and tend to filter out text-heavy pages because of information overload. So even though a text-dense page might be seen as more trustworthy, it tends to get less attention from youth because of the cognitive demands. However, as youth gain experience navigating online texts, their ability to discern the quality of texts improves. More sophisticated online youth have identified markers of quality as including citations, coherency, and evidence of editing.

SUGGESTIONS FOR TEACHING

There are numerous articles and lessons available that discuss ways of teaching youth how to identify trustworthy online texts. The most effective, perhaps, are those that help students understand how information is constructed. This can be done by actively engaging students as producers or content creators, which is a role that is consistent with the Web 2.0 world and their place in it.

For instance, students can examine the history page and discussion pages of Wikipedia entries. They can see how the entry changed over time and how people talk about the changes that are made. Students can then use a class wiki to create a compendium of information pertaining to the course they are in and actively track the history of the entries and the accompanying discussions.

Creating a class wiki will require a fair amount of scaffolding. Students at first may be hesitant to change another person's entry beyond a few minor edits. This hesitancy can be addressed by teaching students to accompany each revision with a short posting in the discussion or comments section of the wiki. Over time, students can see how the information evolves and becomes clearer and more accurate. Reviewing the history of the page can show the actual chronology and changes. The comments will show the thought processes behind the changes.

Another approach is being developed by W. Ian O'Byrne (2009), a doctoral student at the University of Connecticut. O'Byrne has students create fake Web pages with false information. By doing so, the students begin to understand what goes into creating a Web page and how easy it is to create something that looks credible even if it is not. This approach is more intensive than examining wiki histories and creating a class wiki, but it holds promise for teaching a wide range of skills as well as critical media literacy.

IDENTIFYING QUALITY STUDENT WRITING

Like identifying quality texts to read, identifying quality student work has typically been a top-down endeavor done through rubrics or scoring guides created by teachers, building and district leaders, the state, textbook publishers, or testing companies. However, in a Web 2.0 world, quality is determined from the ground up. In this section, we will consider what constitutes quality writing and how we can leverage the collaborative nature of Generation 2.0 to support the application of a jointly constructed understanding of good writing to their development as writers.

THE ROLE OF AUDIENCE AND PURPOSE

One of the foundations of being a writer or teaching writing is understanding that how one writes is dependent upon the targeted audience and the purpose of the writing. This perspective is consistent with the view that literacy is a social act—that we use texts for purposes that make sense within the social groups to which we belong. This is true whether the text is an essay written in ink on paper, a movie to be distributed via the Internet, or a sophisticated multimedia project that spans different modes of delivery. In understanding composition or text production as a social act, we must also consider the roles of context, audience, and authenticity. Whether a text meets the needs of the audience in the context within which it is being used determines whether it is considered a quality text.

Context

We must remember that there are several differences between writing traditional texts for school purposes and writing for the larger world using digital tools. First, writing done for a school-based essay and writing done online or using social media such as texting or a social networking site have radically different contexts.

Context refers to the circumstances within which a person is writing or reading, why they are writing or reading, and with whom. Context affects what a person knows and believes about a text. For instance, someone sending and receiving a text most likely knows the background information about the sender and the content of the text, so less information needs to be explained in the actual message. The sender is also sending the text for a very specific reason, even if it is just to keep the receiver aware of his or her presence. A high level of background knowledge can also be held for youth who write fanfiction. Those who write and read fanfiction share knowledge of the characters and setting in which the fanfiction exists. They also share the purpose of writing and reading each other's writing for pleasure as well as developing their skills in writing.

On the other hand, school-based writing, such as essays, is said to be decontextualized. In reality, school-based writing is highly contextualized, and the context is school. Writing done for school is done for an amorphous audience or a "pretend" audience dictated by the assignment. Therefore, the writer has to guess what the supposed reader of the text knows. As such, the rules of school-based writing include the assumption that the reader has very little background knowledge about the situation and therefore more must be explained. The purpose of school-based writing is usually evaluation or assessment, even if the writing prompt directs that the piece is persuasive or informative. In reality, in the context of school, the student knows that the essay really is not going to persuade or inform anyone and is being used to demonstrate that the student knows the features of a persuasive or informative essay.

The issue of context or knowing/not knowing one's audience and the purpose of the piece of writing lies at the heart of some of the difficulties youth experience with academic writing. Having grown adept at using the tools of the new literacies for communicating with friends and participating in online communities, youth may struggle with the decontextualized nature of academic writing. However, explicit instruction in and discussion about who the audience really is in an academic setting will help youth make the transition from one type of text production to another. For instance, when writing a persuasive essay, students should be instructed to make all aspects of their argument explicit rather than assuming the reader has the requisite background knowledge.

Students should be taught that their audience is, in fact, a real person—a test reader—who has a particular set of expectations about the piece of writing he or she will receive from the student. In some cases the reader may be the teacher, whom the student knows, and in other cases it is an unknown reader appointed by the school, district, state, or testing organization (such as in the SAT or AP tests). In either case, the student needs to be taught that his or her writing needs to assume the audience will only draw on what is in the text and not on knowledge of the writer.

Audience

The issue of audience is, in fact, the second major difference between school-based writing and writing within the new literacies. Audience in the new literacies is more than just knowing who is receiving your text. Being an audience member also implies active engagement or participation in the creation of and use of the text, rather than just being a passive recipient of a text created by an unknown person.

Youth who are engaged in digital literacies may understand this aspect of audience even better than their teachers, who may be less familiar with participatory culture. Therefore, rather than being seen as a distraction, the digital literacies of people like Lisa and Joaquín can be seen as a foundation for helping students hone their sense of audience and purpose, learn to adjust their writing to fit accordingly, and for understanding that reading and writing are actually a transaction between reader and writer rather than being a one-way street. That is, students will know that they have to adjust multiple elements of their texts to fit their intended recipients. This can be a powerful place to begin writing instruction.

Authenticity

Yet another difference between writing within the new literacies and school-based writing is the issue of authenticity. It has become axiomatic to tell teachers to create "authentic" assignments with real purposes and real audiences. The Internet is being extolled as a place where youth can publish their writing so that people beyond the four walls of the school can see what they are doing. The participatory Web holds promise that youth can use their writing to reach out to the world and maybe even make a difference. This all sounds wonderful, but in reality it is much harder to hold the attention of youth and to engage them in these types of activities. Simply assigning a blog or media project will not automatically create an authentic reason to create texts.

Instead, the participatory culture and collaborative nature of Generation 2.0 tells us that we need to tap into communities in which youth are already engaged and then guide them to develop ways to further their membership in those communities. It is this type of connection that helped Lisa develop as a writer. Because her family and friends intended to go to college, doing well in school and on school-based writing assignments connected her to her friends and family. For Joaquín, the new literacies of making beats and creating videos helped him maintain his connection to Dominican culture and the Spanish language, all the while building a sense of accomplishment among his peers and within school.

It is also important to recognize that writing for school or a test is actually an authentic task with a real audience and purpose. Although the activities done for school have often been called decontextualized or disconnected from real life, school activities have a place in society. Conversations should be held with the students to discuss who the readers are and what their expectations are for the text. A discussion about how particular ways of spelling, word selection, or organization send a message to the text reader can help the students understand who their audience is and how best to adjust their writing to the needs of that audience.

DETERMINING QUALITY IN A WEB 2.0 WORLD

As previously discussed, in traditional educational settings, quality is determined by experts (such as teachers) and measured by rubrics or other evaluation techniques. In a Web 2.0 world, quality is determined by the masses through mechanisms such as page hits, links, comments, and ratings. For instance, even though a fan page for a celebrity may not meet the standards of an essay for English, if it draws the attention of a significant number of people, it can be said that the Web page meets some measure of quality if quality is measured by the ability to draw attention. A Web page can also be said to meet the quality requirements of its audience if many people link to it from their blogs or Web pages. A posting on Facebook or a blog can also be said to meet the quality requirements of the audience if many people comment on the post. Finally and most obviously, the quality of a person's contribution is determined by rating systems built into different online communities.

Multiple online communities have rating systems in place. YouTube allows registered users to rate videos. Amazon.com, among many other online retailers, invites users to rate and review the items they have purchased and allows people to rate these reviews. Not only is the product being rated, the quality of the review is also being rated.

Thus, the idea of evaluation is nothing new to students; however, they may not see how the grassroots rating system in place online can be used in the school environment, which is used to a top-down system. Therefore, some "deprogramming" may be needed.

In order to accomplish this deprogramming, multiple lessons may be needed to first identify what constitutes a quality piece of writing within the school community. This requires honest and open input from the teacher about the nature of education and the evaluation system. Teachers need to help students demystify the way grades are assigned to written work within the various disciplines. Taking this step requires a bit of bravery and an act of faith on the part of the teacher.

SUGGESTED ACTIVITY

1. Either as a whole group or in small groups, examine various YouTube videos and the ratings posted for those videos. Have students explain why they think the different YouTube members rated the videos as they did. As a class, develop a set of qualities students believe make for a quality video.
2. Either as a whole group or in small groups, examine reviews written on various sites such as Amazon.com. Consider the ratings those reviews received. Discuss why those reviews possibly received the ratings they did. What makes a review useful? As a class, develop a set of qualities students believe make for a useful review.
3. Have students read a variety of blogs or online articles on subjects in which students express interest. The students should also read the comments that follow the blogs or articles. As a whole class or in small groups, discuss what made the article worth commenting on. Discuss the usefulness of the comments. How do the comments serve to add to the conversation about the subject?

   • As a class, develop a set of qualities students believe make for an article worth commenting on.
   • As a class, develop a set of qualities students believe make for meaningful comments.

4. Have the students compare the different sets of qualities they identified. What qualities exist across genres? Where are there differences?
5. Examine the rubrics commonly used for assessing school-based essays (use the tools most commonly used in your content area). Compare the qualities identified by the rubric with the qualities the students identified. What qualities exist across contexts? Where are there differences?
6. As a class, use the shared qualities to create a common rubric for writing. When assigning any writing, review these qualities, and as a class, develop any qualities that are unique to the assignment.

Although this activity may take a fair amount of time, the learning that occurs during the activity will support future writing. As such, subsequent writing assignments will require less general instruction as the year progresses, thus freeing up time for focused instruction on new material and skills. Furthermore, this sequential activity builds on the collaborative nature of Generation 2.0, builds on the participatory nature of the Web 2.0 world, and taps into the ways of thinking required as part of the twenty-first-century skills.

SUMMARY

Traditionally in schools and in the predigital world, the quality of texts was determined by experts. Members of Generation 2.0, however, are used to a world where quality is determined collectively through processes such as comments and online rankings. For Generation 2.0, text quality is affected by many features such as the amount of text, the design of the page, and the use of illustrations and color, as well as traditional concerns such as citations, coherency, and evidence of editing. With this understanding in mind, the teacher can use the collaborative nature of Generation 2.0 to explore and determine the quality of texts that will be read and created in the classroom.

One way teachers can build student understanding of quality writing is to work with students to analyze the quality of online media resources such as Wikipedia. Students can be guided to create their own version of Wikipedia or fake websites as well, in order to understand how online resources are created.

A number of issues must be considered when determining the quality of the text. Does it meet the needs of the audience? This should be carefully considered, especially since "audience" in the Web 2.0 world implies participation rather than just consumption of the text. Does the text serve its purpose within the community it is intended for? Does it meet the requirements of the community? These factors are the same whether the text is an ink-and-paper text or an online multimodal text. However, multimodal texts are part of a conversation and thus are rated by number of links, actual page ratings, and the comments received.

The collaborative act of determining quality takes more time than the top-down approach of using a rubric developed by the teacher or an outside service, but by taking the time to build consensus on the definition of a quality text, students are learning both how to read critically and how to construct texts that will allow them to join in the conversation.

Part II

APPLYING THE WORLD OF GENERATION 2.0 TO WRITING INSTRUCTION

Chapter Five

Rethinking the Research Paper

One of the toughest challenges facing teachers as a result of digital technologies is that they are forcing us to rethink how people learn. As discussed earlier in this book, through formal educational settings we have come to accept that people learn by having experts share bits and pieces of knowledge as determined appropriate by the experts for the stage of the learner. For example, with younger children, Piaget's model of development informed the type of activities that were deemed appropriate for particular ages. More recently, application of the theories initially developed by Vygotsky (1978) has led to teachers thinking about communities of learners, zones of proximal development, and scaffolding. Specifically, teachers now consider how they can guide students to new levels of understandings and skills rather than waiting for a developmental level to be reached and a mental switch to be flicked.

In the Vygotskian (or neo-Vygotskian) model, learning occurs within the zone of proximal development, or the moment when learners are presented with a task they cannot accomplish on their own, but can with the assistance of an expert. For instance, a young child cannot tie his or her shoe alone, but can with a parent guiding his or her movements. As the child gains facility in the task, the parent withdraws support until the child is able to accomplish the task alone and eventually become an expert in his or her own right.

Another key element of this type of learning is that the tasks being learned have value within the community. The learner not only learns skills, but also learns how to be a productive member of the community. Of course, this way of learning is not new. It is, in fact, how people within agrarian communities learn, how children within families learn, and how craftspeople and people in the skilled trades learn.

The emergence of Web 2.0 and participatory culture has brought the idea of apprenticeship as a form of learning back into the spotlight and has expanded it beyond its agrarian and crafts-based roots. Now the expert can be anyone of any age, and expertise can be tapped by connecting to an online community. Experts are no longer limited to those who live geographically near, and expertise is no longer determined by a top-down set of credentials (such as a degree or certificate) but instead by demonstrated ability. In other words, learning in the participatory culture of the Web 2.0 world is assessed by performance, an authentic assessment method educators have long talked about but find difficult to implement.

THE RESEARCH PAPER AS A NEW MODEL OF LEARNING

If learning occurs through participation and apprenticing, what does this mean for classroom instruction? Let us start with an experience common in most secondary schools in the United States: writing the research paper. The traditional and somewhat old-style way of guiding students through a research paper includes the following steps:

1. Students select a topic (often from a list provided by the teacher).
2. Students are taken to the library and are given a lesson by the library teacher on what resources are available for their use.
3. Students pull resources (as many as required by the teacher) and take notes (often on index cards).
4. The index cards are sorted and used to create an outline.
5. The outline is used to guide the writing of the paper.
6. A draft is handed in along with the index cards and outline to be checked by the teacher.
7. The teacher returns the draft with feedback, which the student uses for revision.
8. The student hands in the final draft along with the earlier draft, index cards, and outline.

Success is assessed through the use of rubrics or checklists, which may include the number of sources required, the type of sources, the number of index cards required, citation style required, number of pages, format, organization, and so on.

For Generation 2.0, this process needs to be changed.

FROM NOTE TAKING, OUTLINING, AND DRAFTING TO CONTENT CREATION

One of the major changes experienced by Generation 2.0 as a result of Web 2.0 technologies is the movement from being simply content consumers to content producers or creators. Creation is not to be confused with creativity. Content creation can be simple and prosaic—such as posting one's status on a social networking site. What makes it content creation is that the one act, no matter how small, contributes to the overall big picture or collective intelligence of the larger community.

For instance, a young woman may post that she is excited about the upcoming premier of one of the popular *Twilight* movies. This posting by itself does not mean a lot, but when combined with the responses of her friends who comment on her post, as well as postings of other people about their anticipation about the upcoming movie, a larger sense of what the movie means to a segment of youth is developed. The power of this collective sense of what youth are thinking about is evident in the way it is being tapped into by marketing organizations.

Tagging is another case of content being created through the collection of tiny acts. In tagging, a person labels something that is online. Tags can be applied to videos, podcasts, blog postings, pictures, and so on. Whether and how items are tagged depends on the specific platform. What happens is that as multiple people tag items, the software keeps track of those tags. When more than one person tags something with the same label, a sort of "folksonomy," or taxonomy created by ordinary people, is created. Once those tags are established, people can then select the tag to see what items fall under that label.

Content creation also includes more creative acts such as the production and dissemination of videos through sites such as YouTube or Vimeo, or blog postings or fanfiction. These forms of content creation are more involved than tagging or status postings and do in fact become creative acts rather than just acts of content creation. These creative acts, however, are not content until they are posted and disseminated via the Internet. Content creation then hinges on the act of sharing, which in turn makes the person who produced the content part of a community and a participant in a sort of public conversation.

WHY CONTENT CREATION IS IMPORTANT

Jenkins (2006) argues that the switch from youth being solely content consumers to content producers is important because through content creation youth are learning a set of skills that are needed to do well in today's fast-paced, information-based society. The skills identified by Jenkins include

- The willingness to experiment as a way to solve problems
- The ability to learn from simulations
- The desire and ability to collaborate
- The ability to draw on multiple tools to develop knowledge
- The knowledge to judge various sources of information
- The ability to adjust one's interactional style in order to best work within a particular group of people or community
- The ability to follow a narrative across multiple modalities
- The ability to perform different roles based on the needs of the community or context of the situation
- The ability to draw from a variety of sources to create something new
- The ability to multitask
- The knowledge of how to search for, synthesize, and disseminate information

A number of these skills have already been discussed in this book. At this point, it is useful to consider the ones not yet discussed that connect directly to the task of writing the research paper. These include using multiple tools to develop knowledge, following a narrative across multiple modalities, drawing from different sources to create something new, and the knowledge of how to search for, synthesize, and disseminate information.

TOPIC SELECTION

For Generation 2.0, the research paper writing process should look quite different from the traditional model. First, consider topic selection. Whereas in the traditional model, topics are selected from a list provided by the teacher, in a Web 2.0 world, topics could be developed out of communities youth are already engaged in and where they have already been established as apprentice learners.

Mizuko (Mimi) Ito and her team of researchers from the University of California (2008) argue that the "hanging out" that youth do online is the first step in gaining skills in various digital activities. As interest grows, youth move from "hanging out" to "messing around," which involves playing with whatever digital tool is central to the online world in which they are engaged.

Black's (2005) work on fanfiction as well as Chandler-Olcott and Mahar's (2003) description of anime production provides a clear example of how this works. These authors show how some youth are initially enamored by a particular text or genre such as anime (Japanese animation with stylized artwork and characters) and *manga* (Japanese graphic novels with the same aesthetic as anime). They may be voracious readers of manga and spend hours "hanging out" watching anime online or reading manga. They might then move on to remixing anime and uploading a few clips of their own, or in the case of Black's research, the youth might use the characters as a springboard for their own stories, which they post online.

As students move from hanging out to messing around, the youth are learning the tools of video or text production, and learning what makes a video worth watching or a story worth reading, as well as what kinds of feedback from other members of the community are helpful. In other words, they are learning how to be members of a community and developing skills valued by members of that community by collaborating and apprenticing with other members of the community.

For a few young people, the next step of "geeking out" follows. These are the people who become intrigued by the technology and the community and move not only toward engagement with the community but also toward developing recognized expertise in that community. They move from just playing around with the technology to learning more about it by establishing relationships with people already in the community, asking questions, and posting their own work and soliciting feedback on a fairly consistent basis. The important point is that it is a community of their choosing and the information they are seeking is meaningful to their membership in the community. Furthermore, as they "geek out" they are working within their zone of proximal development and are accomplishing things they could not on their own.

How then to leverage the apprenticeship model and youth community membership for something like a research paper?

Rather than starting with a preset list of topics, teachers could find out the "hanging out" activities their students are engaged in. Using those as the starting point, the teacher and the community can help the students make connections to the course content. For example, a fan of Stephenie Meyer's *Twilight* series could research the historical origins of vampirism for a global studies class, the literary history of vampires for an English class, or symbiosis, parasites, blood-borne diseases, decay, and so on for a life science class.

Rather than having the teacher guide the question, however, the teacher can provide the overall objective and then have the student turn to the fan community for ideas on what might be interesting to learn about. In other words, rather than going into the project with the topic already set in stone, the student can surf within the online world he or she is already familiar with, seeking connections to the course content. The key is that the teacher, the student, and the community work together to find an imaginative topic that is compelling enough to move the student from the "hanging out" stage to the "messing around" stage, where they want to learn more.

A word of warning must be given here, however. Care must be taken not to ruin the topic for the student by turning it into an onerous task rather than one of pleasurable discovery. Turning a teen's obsession with *Twilight* into a series of assignments or tasks that have to be checked off a rubric is sure to either ruin the reading experience for the student or result in resistance from the student. The student needs to be allowed to play or "mess around" with the ideas with the understanding that he or she will make the connections to the academic piece in time. This may seem to be a contradiction to the way research is currently approached in schools, but in reality it is the way master's and doctoral theses are developed. The passion comes first; the intellectual exploration develops from there.

SUMMARY

The new literacies have forced teachers to rethink how people learn and what it means to research and write. They have reinvigorated the apprenticeship model of learning and have made apparent how even older students move through zones of proximal development when learning digital skills through membership in an online community. Rethinking the research paper, which is part of the curriculum in many secondary schools, is a way to see how the new literacies are changing the nature of writing instruction and learning.

The old linear model of conducting research and writing papers is insufficient for Generation 2.0. Using the tools of Web 2.0, students can take the research paper beyond the walls of the classroom into the communities and affinity groups in which they are members. The research paper can be used to guide students toward being content creators rather than simply consumers. Membership in affinity groups and communities can be used to guide topic selection, which can then lead to additional learning.

Chapter Six

Information Gathering

Once a topic has been selected, the next stage is information gathering. First, we need to remember that if the student has selected a topic that is connected to a community in which he or she is already a member, the student already has a sense of what material is available. The skill to be taught in such a situation is sorting out the useful and trustworthy from less trustworthy or less useful sites. These strategies have already been discussed in chapter 4, on what constitutes good writing. The second task is guiding the student to moving beyond what he or she already knows.

Research tells us that members of Generation 2.0 approach information gathering or research in a very different way than their predecessors. It has become almost axiomatic that the first step to research is going online rather than going to the library, and going online means using Google. If this is the case, then teaching information retrieval means teaching students how to select useful keywords and how to come up with synonyms when initial searches result in too many or too few results. The act of seeking information through the use of keywords can be used as an authentic purpose for teaching vocabulary. There are many lessons that can be done to support student development of vocabulary, and some ideas are discussed in chapter 9, on spelling and vocabulary.

We need to remember that members of Generation 2.0 have a different way of thinking about and interacting with information than those of us who grew up prior to the Web 2.0 world. Generation 2.0 is used to a constant flow of information. This information is received throughout the day via status updates on their social networking sites, texts on their cell phones, and possibly Really Simple Syndication (RSS) feeds via something like Google Reader. As discussed in chapter 3 on multitasking, one of the challenges youth face is deciding where to turn their attention in order to make sense of all this information.

The research on information overload tells us that people respond to the steady flow of information by selectively choosing what to pay attention to and what to ignore. In order to make these decisions, youth engage in what Palfrey and Gasser (2008) describe as a three-step process:

1. Grazing. People check posts, blogs, feeds, and texts frequently throughout the day. These pieces of information must be easily accessible and sorted so the focus can be easily identified, timely, relevant, and easy to process. These resources tend to be superficial, and little effort is required to make sense of the information. It is this grazing that we can use to help students select their topic of interest and to lead them into their initial exploration of a topic.
2. Deep dive. If something in this news feed captures an individual's interest, the person then does a "deep dive." At this point, the individual turns to more formal institutions such as official news outlets to gather in-depth information. This is where more guidance is required. Deep dives require knowledge of the type of information that is available, how to find that information by using keywords and synonyms, and how to determine what constitutes a quality text.
3. Engagement. The final step is engagement or participation. Not everyone engages in this step, but on occasion, if people are strongly affected by what they learned through their research, they might comment on the blog or article or write about it themselves in a blog of their own, create a video response, or simply pass the information on to their friends by posting links on their social networking site. The important point is that when an individual takes this step, he or she is contributing to the online conversation about the topic and moves from being a content consumer to being a content creator.

It is the act of participation that connects to the research paper. This is where the student is making sense of the information gathered and is disseminating his or her take on the issue to the larger community. Whereas a traditional research paper ends at the teacher's desk, or maybe with a presentation in front of the class, in the Web 2.0 world, research might end with the public posting of a new understanding of or stance toward the issue. In fact, it could be said that the research is just beginning at this point because the student is now part of a larger conversation about the issue.

AN EXAMPLE

Let us return to the example of the young person who is a fan of the *Twilight* series. If she has a Facebook page, she might have selected "Like" on the

Twilight Saga Facebook page. As a result, her Facebook news feed will show information about the *Twilight Saga* whenever information is added to the page. This is part of the student's grazing. She does not have to make any effort to find the information. It just appears on her Facebook feed. It appears as soon as it is posted, so it is timely, and it is easy to process because it is short and contains only the most relevant information.

If the posting piques the interest of the student—for instance, an announcement about the casting of the latest movie—she can go to a variety of websites for details. If she finds that information to be compelling, she might repost it so that her friends can learn about it, or if there is something she feels the need to comment about (such as disagreeing with the casting), she can post and comment, thus starting a conversation; she could comment on other people's blogs, comments on articles about the casting, or even write her own blog about the event. Granted, her particular contribution may be small and easily overlooked or seen as trivial, but when taken as a whole, this engagement in something that matters to a group of people creates a trend or buzz that people in the movie industry, in this case, pay attention to.

ORGANIZING MULTIPLE INFORMATION SOURCES

Once the student has a topic and plan for gathering information, the next step is compiling the information. Note cards used to be the tool of choice for this task because they could be easily sorted by theme, thus scaffolding the organization of the paper. Teachers would also use the index cards to teach students how to cite where the information came from and to build the bibliography or reference list. These steps can be replaced and enhanced by using blogs. Blogs are essentially online journals that consist of dated entries arranged in reverse chronological order.

Stylistically, blogs are written in an informal and personal voice, but they do tend to follow more formal writing conventions than a posting on a social networking site such as Facebook or MySpace. Blogs range from the highly personal to the political. There are a number of simple-to-use sites that host blogs for free. The most significant aspects of blogs are that they exist within public space (although they can be set to "private" so that only select people may read them), are personal in nature, are a form of publishing, and are characterized by the connections between the blog and other online texts. Finally, blogs are notable because they become part of a conversation by virtue of people commenting on them and linking to them.

Blogs have several advantages over the old method of note cards or notebooks. These advantages include hyperlinking; embedding of images, videos, and audio; and tagging. Other advantages include a built-in expectation for comments or feedback, not only from the teacher but from other members of the community to which the student belongs. Before we turn our attention to using blogs, however, it is worthwhile to rethink the act of note taking.

NOTE TAKING, SUMMARY, AND PARAPHRASING

Note Taking

For inexperienced researchers and writers, note taking during reading often consists of copying quotes directly from the text. More experienced students might paraphrase. It is typically only the most experienced student or researcher who is able to turn the note-taking process into a more meaningful activity by engaging in summary and analysis.

This is where the art of teaching strategic reading and writing is important. Students should be explicitly taught the skills of identifying the main idea, summarizing, and paraphrasing. Bean, Drenk, and Lee's (1982) work on microthemes and Richard Lanham's (2006) paramedic method of tightening writing are particularly helpful here. Microthemes are short (100- to 200-word) writing pieces that require a great deal of thinking. Because they are short and contain focused information, microthemes are less intimidating to students than other writing assignments. Microthemes also allow the teacher to quickly assess what a student is pulling out of a piece of text. Paraphrasing is the act of taking someone else's ideas and putting them into one's own words. In order to summarize and paraphrase accurately, the reader must have a firm idea of the ideas put forth by the writer.

There are four types of microthemes: the summary microtheme, the thesis-support microtheme, the data-provided microtheme, and the quandary-posing microtheme. Here we examine the summary microtheme, as it is the most useful for this phase of the research paper.

The Summary Microtheme

According to the National Commission on Writing (2003), summary writing is one of the skills most essential for writing development. However, summary is a difficult skill to teach students because they often end up retelling rather than summarizing. Thus explicit instruction in summary writing is necessary, and summary microthemes are a helpful approach for teaching the skill.

When writing the summary microtheme, the reader looks for the transitions and other word clues that show how the ideas within the text are related. In other words, the reader must figure out what is the main idea, what are the subordinate ideas, and what are the supporting details. The reader then becomes a writer by condensing the text into its main and subordinating ideas, while leaving out the details. Personal response to the text should be kept separate from the summary. Students can respond to the text by using the comments function of the blog to capture their thinking, or they can create a separate blog post that responds to the text.

The microthemes should be posted on the students' blogs. Hyperlinks to the original articles or websites should be included. Students can use the comments to capture what other members of their community are thinking about that issue. Students should also tag the entries in order to indicate what the gist or central idea of the text was. The summary microthemes will allow students to explore multiple perspectives on an issue without getting distracted by their personal response to the issue. As their ideas begin to gel, students can be taught to write thesis-support microthemes, which are discussed later in this book, in order to bring form to their ideas.

Paraphrasing

Paraphrasing is different from summarizing in that the student is taking what the author has written and is putting it into his or her own words. When paraphrasing, the student writer is not trying to capture the overall gist of the text nor the hierarchies of ideas within a text. Paraphrasing is an important skill, especially for helping students make sense of a difficult passage, and allows them to demonstrate their understanding of that passage.

Although developed as a tool for teaching students to tighten their own writing, Lanham's (2006) paramedic method is a useful tool for parsing or breaking down difficult passages and creating a paraphrase. The method involves the following steps:

1. Circle the prepositions (*of, in, about, for, onto, into,* etc.).
2. Draw a box around the "is" verb forms.
3. Ask, "Where's the action?"
4. Change the "action" into a simple verb.
5. Move the doer into the subject (who is doing what to whom).
6. Eliminate any unnecessary slow wind-ups.
7. Eliminate any redundancies.

For example, the following is the first sentence of the Wikipedia entry on vampires.

Vampires are mythological or folkloric beings who subsist by feeding on the life essence (generally in the form of blood) of living creatures, regardless of whether they are undead or a living person.

This sentence could be paraphrased into "In myths and legends, vampires [the 'who'] feed [the active verb] on blood [the 'whom']." This method shows that many of the prepositional phrases serve only to add detail. For instance, "in the form of blood of living creatures" is redundant because only living creatures have blood. Thus that phrase can be reduced to "feed on blood" or even "consume blood," if we wanted to get rid of the preposition "on." "Vampires are mythological or folkloric beings" can be simplified to "In myths and legends" or "Mythical and legendary vampires." The final phrase of the Wikipedia entry, "regardless of whether they are undead or a living person," can be eliminated since it does not add meaningful information and is actually unclear. The reader is left wondering whether the "they" in the phrase refers to the vampire (whom people often call the "undead") or the victim.

The final piece to teaching paraphrasing is to make sure the students understand that even when they are paraphrasing, they still must cite where the information came from. This concept can be initially learned and reinforced through the practice of hyperlinking.

Hyperlinking

Hyperlinks allow the reader to jump to a new online text simply by clicking on a selected word, phrase, or image. Using hyperlinks in a blog supports students in making text-to-text and text-to-world connections as they write about what they are reading. Hyperlinks also serve as a form of citation. Whereas in traditional texts, sources must be cited in order to give credit to the original authors and to direct the reader to the original text, in a text such as a blog, a hyperlink serves the same purpose. With a click, the reader can go to the original text. Helping students understand the role of hyperlinks in connecting texts to one another can help address issues of plagiarism that often occur in student writing. The issue of plagiarism and the cut-and-paste mentality of Generation 2.0 is discussed in more detail in the section on remixing and plagiarism in chapter 7.

To make the use of blogging and linking most effective, students can be taught to open multiple browser windows or tabs as they are reading a text online. This act appeals to their desire to multitask and also helps alleviate some of the drudgery of reading and note taking. As they are reading, they can go to their blog and take notes about or reflect on what they are reading. The temptation for youth, however, is to simply copy and paste text from the text to the blog.

Quoting, Citing, and Hyperlinks

Students can be taught to use the "quote" style function of many blogs, which they can use to set off direct quotes whenever they do copy and paste from elsewhere. Students can also be taught about citation as they are doing this collection and reflection. Students struggle with the format of citation, whether MLA, APA, Turabian, or Chicago style, and thus tend to resist using citations. By first introducing students to the idea of hyperlinks as citation, teachers can move students through their zone of proximal development in learning academic form. Specifically, allowing them to first use hyperlinks teaches them the concept of citation without the cognitive overload of learning complex formatting at the same time. Once students are comfortable with the concept of citation, the desired style guidelines for the formal research paper can be introduced.

Using hyperlinks can also be used to support text-to-text and text-to-world connections. If the text reminds students of something else they have read or viewed, they can easily find the text online through a search engine and insert the hyperlink into the blog posting. If the text they are thinking of is a graphic or illustration, video, or even audio, they may even be able to embed the text into the blog, further enriching the experience for the blog reader and assisting the students as they compile the information for a formal research paper.

Embedded Graphics, Video, and Audio

Blogs also have the capacity for embedding images or graphics, video, and even audio. This requires a little bit more technical know-how than simply writing text or even adding hyperlinks, but encouraging students to play with the technology and teach others will support learning the technology. The more important aspect is understanding when to embed different texts into a blog to support comprehension.

For example, students researching a scientific or mathematical concept could embed a video or illustration that illustrates the concept. They could also accompany the video or illustration with explanatory text. A student researching an author could embed a picture of the author or even a podcast of a reading from one of the author's poems, novels, or short stories. A student conducting research for a social studies class could embed videos about an event (such as current news stories or reenactments, as appropriate), pictures or illustrations that make the event clearer, or even graphs and charts showing connections or causality between events.

These embedded files could be gathered from online sources, in which case hyperlinks to the original site would be provided, or students could add graphics, illustrations, videos, and audio texts that they themselves created.

Tagging

Students can also be taught to use tagging as a way to help them make sense of the information they are collecting and reflecting on. Tags are simply labels—much like the labels teachers used to encourage students to write at the top of an index card. After a post is written, a student can enter any number of tags into the appropriate space on the blog interface. These tags are created by the student based on what he or she understands about the text being discussed in the blog posting.

Posts are connected to each other when they share a tag, thus creating a sort of grassroots taxonomy (called a "folksonomy" in research). If the students add a "tag cloud" to their blog, they can even have a visual representation of the tags they are using, with the most-used tags in larger text. A tag cloud is a more advanced tool for blogs. A quick search on whichever blog tool is being used will provide instructions for creating and adding a tag cloud to a blog. The folksonomy created by tagging and the subsequent visualization through the tag cloud allows students to see patterns across what they are reading. These tags can form the basis of the structure of the final paper.

When it comes time to draft the paper, students can use their tags to organize their ideas. For instance, a student researching vampire lore for an English class might discover that there are different types of vampires based on geographic and cultural differences. He might decide to organize his essay by geographic regions. His task then would be to select the tag for one geographic area (say, American Southwest). All the blog postings that have been tagged American Southwest will appear, and nonrelevant posts will be hidden. The student can then copy and paste from those posts into his word-processing document. He can create a heading for that collection of material such as "Vampire of the American Southwest." He can then repeat that process for the other geographic areas he discovered.

Commenting

Using blogs also taps into the collaborative aspect, in that members of the students' community can read and comment on what they are posting. Thus they gain multiple perspectives on the material. Students should be encouraged to read and comment on one another's blog postings. However, they need to be taught how to comment in constructive ways. This can be done by examining the comments made to popular blogs, videos, and online articles. Students can identify what makes a comment useful and develop their own set of criteria for commenting on their blogs. Blog authors should also be shown that they can delete offensive comments or set their blogs to moderate comments. To moderate comments means that the author reviews the comment before it is made public. This way offensive or inappropriate comments can be prevented from being made public.

As discussed in the section on summary writing, students can also use the comments function to note personal responses to the texts they are documenting in their blogs. The student can then review all the comments written on the topic and take note of recurring themes or emerging changes in his or her thinking as the student moves through the research process.

The teacher can also use the comments function to guide students as they develop skills in summarizing and reflecting on what they are reading. It should be remembered, however, that the comments are public; thus anything the teacher writes should be sensitive to the needs of the student and also fall within the Family Educational Rights and Privacy Act (FERPA). This law prohibits the public posting of grades, so any comments should be strictly in the realm of constructive feedback rather than evaluative. Furthermore, in that the purpose of this type of blogging is to collect and make sense of information, the teacher should attend to content rather than mechanics. Certainly, because the blog is public space, students should be pushed to represent themselves as intelligent and knowledgeable, but given the informal nature of blogging, students should not be penalized for not adhering to the standards of academic writing.

SUMMARY

The way Generation 2.0 gathers information or learns about something is different from previous generations. With the constant flow of information coming in, Generation 2.0's first experience is with information on the surface; when they find something that captures their attention, they do a deep dive to discover more detail. Once youth learn what they wish, they may then move to the third step, which is engagement or participation, where they post comments or create something new with the information.

By using blogging, the research paper can be used as a tool for engagement in a community or affinity group that is important to the student. Blogging connects the student; allows for hyperlinking, the embedding of audio, video, and images, and tagging, which can be used to organize the information; and readers can contribute comments, which serve as a form of feedback. Furthermore, blogging can be used to support the traditional writing-to-learn activities of summary and paraphrasing, as well as the professional practices of citation.

One approach to teaching summary is through the technique of summary microthemes that are posted to the blogs. Summary and personal response should be kept separate through the use of comments or by having the stu-

Chapter Seven

Drafting and Revising

Once the information has been gathered, summarized, reflected on, and organized through the use of a blog, the writer's challenge is making the transition from the informal style of the blog to the formal structure and style of an academic paper. Traditionally, writing is seen as a linear process. Even with the use of the writing process, which acknowledges the recursive nature of writing, most people still approach the actual act of composition in a linear fashion.

Generally, students believe they start writing at the beginning with an introduction, move through the body of the paper, and then end by writing a conclusion. They may stop and start through this process, or go back and check for more information, but typically students begin writing at the beginning and consider the piece done after they have written the conclusion. Some more sophisticated writers may know to write the introduction last or to revise the introduction after they have completed the paper, but nonetheless, students tend to approach the actual writing act as one of "sit down and go." This way of thinking about the actual act of writing is reinforced by on-demand writing tasks such as those required in standardized and mandated tests. Academically successful students necessarily develop the skill to write a "good-enough" paper from start to finish in a limited period of time.

Here though, with something as complex as a research paper, it is more useful to think of the paper as being built rather than written. From this perspective, if the student has done a good job of collecting material on the blog, the task of creating the paper is more than half done. The blog entries constitute the building blocks of the paper, and it becomes the task of the writer to configure them in a way that works and to mortar those bricks together with rhetorical strategies such as transitions.

Another benefit of approaching writing the paper from this perspective is that it is easier to revise than to start from scratch. If a student uses existing blog posts as the starting point, which he or she then copies and pastes into a word-processing document, the student will be amazed at the quantity of text already generated. The task the student then faces is not the frightening empty screen and flashing cursor, but rather the less intimidating task of turning initial ideas into a clear, connected, and coherent argument supported by facts.

The end result of this effort will be a very rough draft of the body of the research paper. The basic information will be in place and the paper will be generally organized. The next step is revising it so that the paper meets the agreed-upon standards of a quality text.

Before discussing revision, however, some time should be spent exploring the issue of plagiarism. This is especially important if the student has copied and pasted material from his or her blog, which may contain text that has been taken from elsewhere. Even if the student has hyperlinked the original text, it is still necessary for the student to learn academic citation practices and to be aware of copyright and fair-use laws.

REMIXING AND PLAGIARISM

A challenge in turning the collection of blog posts into a coherent paper will be the students' desire to simply copy and paste from their blog and call the essay done. Youth who have engaged in what is called remixing are used to this type of composition and understand it as a legitimate creative act. Remixing (sometimes called "mash-up") is a creative act in which people use snippets from existing materials and juxtapose them against other snippets from different sources in ways that create something new. These works are considered "transformative works" because the purpose of the original works has been changed.

Transformative works are legal under copyright laws as long as the author follows the rules of fair use. A well-known and well-done example of remixing is the video mash-up *Buffy versus Edward*, in which the composer/author carefully selected various clips from the television program *Buffy the Vampire Slayer* and clips from the movie *Twilight* in order to make a statement about gender roles and relationships (McIntosh, 2009). The video is available for viewing on YouTube, and the author has also written about the genesis of this project and the composition process. The remix ends with a list of where the clips were taken from, and the composer/author also notes that the remix meets the legal requirements of fair use.

Showing students well-done remixes and discussing issues of fair use can be used as a platform for moving students toward standard citation practices. The list of sources provided at the end of the *Buffy versus Edward* remix can be compared to the reference list or bibliography required at the end of an academic paper. The composition of the video can also be examined in light of fair-use laws.

First, the law requires that new work be sufficiently different from the original so as to be clear that it is a new creative piece. Second, the amount of material taken from the original work(s) should be no more than necessary to accomplish the transformative purpose of the new work. In the case of *Buffy versus Edward*, the composer/author used only those clips necessary for telling the desired story. Third, it must be clear that the new work does not replace the original, which would cause harm to the creator of the original work. The *Buffy versus Edward* video would never be mistaken for or replace either the original *Buffy the Vampire Slayer* episodes or the *Twilight* movie.

AUTHENTIC PURPOSES FOR REVISION

Even if the teacher is able to get the student to summarize, paraphrase, and cite the original texts, as suggested earlier in this book, there remains the challenge of guiding the student to spending time with the revision strategies necessary to make for a smoothly flowing and meaningful paper. There are no answers to this challenge; indeed, it is the same hurdle teachers always have to face when trying to move students from the first draft to the final version.

First, there must be agreement between the students and teacher as to what constitutes a quality text. Therefore, the teacher and students should examine blogs that contain coherent, well-thought-out ideas supported by research. Time should be spent analyzing different bloggers' writing styles and organizational strategies. The teacher and students can continually circle back to the conversations about what constitutes a quality text and use those discussions to form a framework for what the expectations are for the final paper. These recommendations are, of course, no different from what a teacher would do when teaching a traditional essay through the study of exemplars. In this case, however, the exemplars are blogs.

Second, if students are not invested in the paper, they may have little to no desire to expend a great deal of energy on writing. However, students may find themselves more motivated to create a quality text if they have an authentic outlet for the final paper. For example, rather than simply handing the paper in to the teacher, students can post their final paper on the blog. If their friends and members of their community have been following the student as he or she collects information and develops ideas, the final essay will provide the opportunity to share how the student author sees the information as all fitting together.

Another alternative is an online magazine that the class can publish using a wiki. Friends, family, and community members should be invited to view the papers posted. A wiki is essentially a simplified website that members can collaboratively create. Some free wiki services include Pbworks.com and Wikispaces.com. Once the wiki is set up by the teacher, students can be given access to the wiki either as just readers or as writers or editors. The different levels allow the students to do different things on the wiki. As writers or editors, students can add work to the wiki or make changes. Editors have more rights than writers.

The front page of the wiki could be set up as a table of contents, and subsequent pages could be set up as either individual articles or as magazine issues that correspond to each major assignment. Papers could then be uploaded as pdf files and posted on those pages for downloading by interested readers. Depending on how the wiki is set up, the papers could include not just the texts but also multimodal compositions by the students. For example, research papers could be accompanied by the illustrations and graphics that students collected during the research phase of the assignment. Podcasts of the students presenting their papers could also be included, as well as slideshows or links to slideshows. How the wiki is used depends on the creativity and technological skill of the teacher and students. It would be wise, however, to start small with just posting the papers and add modalities as comfort with the technology grows.

THE ACT OF REVISION

The next task is to refine this rough piece into something coherent and meaningful to potential readers. The revision process is about uncovering what the student author sees as the connection between ideas rather than an arbitrary flow of ideas as dictated by a predetermined rubric. Furthermore, we have not yet attended to the introduction, thesis statement, or conclusion. This is because we are approaching the writing of this paper through the process of discovery, experimentation, and playfulness rather than a recitation of facts about a topic or even an attempt to prove a predetermined point. In fact, the student may not know what his or her thesis statement is until after he or she has read the material, thought about it through the prewriting done via blogging or the organizing of the ideas through the use of tagging, and then rethought about it by seeking to connect the ideas through the process of revision.

It is helpful to see this step in the writing process as that of re-visioning or re-seeing rather than revising or cleaning up a draft. It is most certainly different from proofreading, which is about surface errors. Re-visioning involves using the processes of revising (such as seeking clarifying language, selecting precise words, reordering ideas, and integrating transitions) to more fully understand what the author is thinking and what the author wants the reader to understand. When re-visioning, the author is still writing to learn but is doing so with the reader in mind. The author is asking himself or herself, "What do I mean here, and how do I make it clear to my reader?" With re-vision in mind, it is appropriate to turn our attention to the issues of coherence and organization, because those are the two aspects of writing that will best help the author achieve his or her goal at this point.

MICROTHEMES TO SUPPORT RE-VISIONING

Microthemes are focused pieces of 100 to 200 words written by students in response to texts. Although short, microthemes demand a great deal of thinking on the part of the student. Microthemes also allow the teacher to quickly assess the student's grasp of the material. The summary microtheme was discussed earlier in this book. Here we return to the concept of the microtheme but turn our attention to the thesis-support microtheme and the data-provided microtheme.

The Thesis-Support Microtheme

A thesis-support microtheme helps students discover issues and take a stance. This allows the students to take the information they are gathering and pull it together into a focused argument rather than a set of facts or a data dump. In a thesis-support microtheme, students should be taught to write a focused thesis statement and then support it with evidence from the texts they have been reading. The thesis can be developed by examining the comments the students made in response to their summary microthemes.

For example, the student exploring vampire legends in different cultures may have noticed that people are both repelled by and attracted to vampires. She may also have noticed that early works saw vampires as evil, but recent literature has focused on the attractiveness of vampires. Her personal response to vampires, based on her love of the *Twilight Saga,* is that they are sexy. Thus, she might write a thesis-support microtheme along the lines of "Modern American vampires are more attractive than vampires of other cultures and time periods." The thesis-support microtheme is not subtle, but it is effective for teaching students to take a stance that can be argued, and then supporting that stance with evidence from the literature. Once students have practice doing this with microthemes that they post to their blog, they can expand their ideas in their research paper.

The Data-Provided Microtheme

The data-provided microtheme is the opposite of the thesis-support microtheme. In the thesis-support microtheme, the student starts with the stance and finds the material to support the stance. In the data-provided microtheme, the student starts with the data and develops the theme from it. This microtheme is particularly useful in science-based courses where students are asked to review data and come up with conclusions. The writing process is the same, however. Once the student analyzes the data and determines what it means, he or she must make a claim (thesis) and show how the data supports it.

Using microthemes in conjunction with blogging allows students to go beyond simple fact collection to making sense of the information they have collected *as they are collecting it.* If students are encouraged to use the blog as a space to respond to the text rather than simply as a collection tool, they can also be moved away from the copy-and-paste syndrome and the consequent risk of plagiarism.

THE PARAMEDIC METHOD FOR RE-VISIONING

Lanham's (2006) paramedic method for revising prose should also be used. If students have gained comfort and facility with the method as a way of making sense of and paraphrasing the work of others, they can then apply it to their own writing. Students can go on a passive verb hunt and search out prepositional phrases in order to streamline their writing. By doing so, they will also discover areas where they are not quite sure what they were trying to say. This will result not only in clearer writing but also in the clearer, more concise development of ideas. Finally, the paramedic method can be used to ferret out redundancies and empty phrases.

The task of applying the paramedic method to their own writing may raise resistance among students who are used to writing something and being done with it. Too often writing and revision are seen as a task to be quickly done with rather than as the process of exploration and learning; however, if writing is framed by the Generation 2.0 practice of play and experimentation as well as having an authentic audience, resistance may lessen somewhat.

SUMMARY

For Generation 2.0, the act of writing the research paper should be reframed as an act of revising and formalizing what they have created through blogging. In traditional writing instruction, revising typically is seen as onerous and as a last step rather than as a creative act. For Generation 2.0, revision can be seen as an act of remix, mash-up, or the creative use of existing material to make something new. Remixing the materials collected through blogging will result in a rough draft of the paper, which then can be revised to meet the agreed-upon standards for an academic paper.

When approaching drafting and revision through the lens of remix, the teacher needs to explicitly teach students how to avoid the risk of plagiarism that may arise through copy-and-paste practices. Students, however, may resist the effort necessary to adequately revise and cite if they are not invested in the paper. Therefore, authentic audiences must be part of the writing process. Authentic audiences can be found through online communities of bloggers or a class e-zine created using a wiki.

The actual act of drafting revision should be approached as an act of reseeing, discovery, experimentation, and playfulness rather than as a recitation of facts. The use of thesis-support microthemes and data-provided microthemes helps students understand the relation of a text to another text. Through these two microthemes, students also learn to synthesize data and use evidence to support their claim or thesis. Teaching students to write microthemes and posting these themes to blogs can help students move away from the reiteration of facts and toward the creation of new ideas from those facts.

Chapter Eight

Coherence and Organization

Coherence and organization are two concepts within writing that are closely related. In traditional writing forms, organization refers to the overall structure of the text and how the main pieces of a text are ordered. Coherence means that the author constructed the text so that elements of the text, from the individual words to the sentences to the paragraphs, connect and flow. The flow helps the reader easily understand how ideas are connected to one another and to the central idea of the whole text. The fear among educators (and English teachers in particular), is that because digital forms such as instant messaging and texting encourage short bursts of text, or status posts on something like Facebook or MySpace are built on short bursts of texts, youth are not learning how to write lengthy pieces that hold together.

Organization is dictated in part by the genre of the text, as well as by the intended audience and purpose of the piece. For instance, a how-to article follows an organizational structure based on sequence, and historical narratives typically follow a cause-and-effect pattern. Other common organizational patterns are compare and contrast, general to specific, and order of importance. These patterns are often found in informational, persuasive, and argument texts. Paragraphs also tend to be organized in predictable ways such as claim (topic sentence), evidence, and interpretation for argument papers. Furthermore, texts intended for people new to a field are more apt to follow accepted patterns closely than those written for experts who are able to adapt to unexpected organizational patterns.

Coherence is created by grammatical structures that indicate how one word is related to another. Each word in a sentence performs a particular job, and coherence within that sentence is created when each word contributes to the overall meaning of the sentence in a way that makes sense to the reader and is consistent with the intent of the author. The more complex a sentence becomes, the more difficult it is to hold coherence. Therefore, the writer must take care to use rhetorical devices to help the reader. Rhetorical devices include repetition of words, pronouns that have clear references, and connective words such as *and, or, but, however, therefore,* and so on. The same rhetorical tools are used to link sentences within a paragraph. Take a moment to notice the rhetorical tools in this paragraph and ask how they helped you understand what you were reading.

Typically the short bursts of text used by youth when texting, instant messaging, or posting on a social network page are not complex enough to require the use of the rhetorical tools listed above nor do they follow set rules of organization, because the postings or texts are in response to the moment. However, this does not mean that coherence is not a concern. In fact, because youth may be multitasking or engaged in other online conversations, sending texts to multiple people, or checking their social networking site throughout the day, other tools are needed to help the user keep track of what is going on.

Postings and texts must be constructed to stand alone or to contain words that connect the reader to previous postings, texts, or specific events. Furthermore, because youth also may be following a text across multiple modes of communication (such as a television program streamed over the Internet, a website or blog about the program, and a fan page on Facebook, as well as postings and conversations by friends), they need to develop new ways to understand how a narrative holds together. Jenkins (2006) calls this skill "transmedia navigation."

In order to navigate across media, readers/viewers need to remember aspects of other texts and access those memories when they encounter references to those texts in different modes and media platforms. For instance, if they come to know a character from a movie and then see that character again in a video game, they draw on their knowledge of what that character represents based on the movie in order to know how to interact with it in the video game. A song or sample from a song might also act in the same way.

Hyperlinks also change the notion of organization and coherency. In a traditional ink-and-paper text, how the reader moves through a text is more or less controlled by the writer. The writer decides the order in which a reader encounters the ideas. Of course, a reader may choose to skip parts of a text, read one section or chapter before another, or just dip into a text to pull out a particular piece of information. This sampling of a text is more likely with informational texts than with narratives. In fact, editors design reference books to be read selectively.

Hyperlinks, however, take the idea of sampling a text one step further. In a traditional ink-and-paper text, even when the reader picks and chooses what to read, he or she is still limited by what the author has chosen to include. In a hyperlinked text, the reader can veer off into any number of directions, some intended by the author, but others not. Coherency and organization within a hyperlinked text is maintained not just through the rhetorical devices discussed earlier in this section, but also through the author's selection of which hyperlinks to include. However, when the reader leaves the path designed by the author, the problem of organization and coherency no longer resides with the author and instead becomes the responsibility of the reader.

Therefore, it is not that youth do not understand the concepts of organization and coherency; it may be that they may have a different notion of what makes something hold together. Organization and coherency for Generation 2.0 may be less about how one word, sentence, or paragraph works in relation to another word, sentence, or paragraph but more about how one word, sentence, hyperlink, image, sound, or piece of music evokes or points to another. They may, in fact, be more sensitive to the concept of intertextuality, or how one text refers to another, than previous generations. This sense of how texts are dependent upon one another for meaning making can therefore be used as a springboard for teaching how the elements within traditional texts are dependent upon one another for meaning.

TEACHING ORGANIZATION AND COHERENCE

Learning to write well-organized and coherent texts is challenging and requires multiple experiences over the lifetime of a writer. However, there are basic lessons that tap into youths' knowledge of audience and purpose, as well as the innate sense of rhetorical structures they learn from engagement in the new literacies.

Sentence Coherence

Sentences must be coherent. Every word within a sentence must relate to the other words in the sentence. Furthermore, sentences must contain all the necessary information in order for the sentence to make sense. When a sentence lacks all the information, we often refer to those sentences as "incomplete" or "fragments." Sentences in which each word does not relate to the other words in the sentence are often identified as "awkward." Those terms, however, tend to be meaningless to students. Instead, it is more worthwhile to use what students know about texting and status postings to build their understanding of what makes complete and coherent sentences.

One approach is to ask students to share messages they have recently sent using their cell phone or posted on their social networking site. Remind them that these messages should be appropriate for school, not hurtful toward any person, and not revealing of personal information. These messages can then be analyzed to show how they contain complete ideas, or how the writer had to follow up with additional text in order to make an idea complete. Rather than discussing subjects and predicates, teachers can demonstrate that complete messages contain an actor and action—in other words, who is doing what.

Another approach is to use lift sentences from student writing (names should be removed) and present them to students as if each sentence or chunk of the sentence is part of an online conversation. Rather than asking students what is missing or what is wrong with a sentence, a teacher can ask students what the sentence means and what further information they need in order to understand the sentence better.

Once students see that each message they create contains all the pieces of a complete sentence, they can then be shown how subsequent messages contribute additional information. This understanding can then be used to move students through sentence-combining activities and the construction of compound, complex, and compound-complex sentences containing a variety of clauses and phrases. The paramedic method discussed earlier can be used to show how to clarify confusing sentences. If students are taught to see each sentence they write as similar to an "utterance" in a text message exchange, they can begin to grasp the idea that each sentence must contain a full thought that is understandable to their audience.

Only examples that show what the students already know or are capable of doing should be discussed. The teacher should not use snippets of student-produced text to highlight "bad grammar" or misspellings. Anything contributed by students should be treated with respect and as worthy of serious consideration. Casual student writing should *never* be the subject of ridicule or scorn in the classroom or even in conversation with colleagues.

Building from what the students know and are able to do with language is more effective than teaching discrete parts of language in decontextualized grammar lessons. Many students can parrot bits of grammatical knowledge such as the definition of a noun or verb, even as they continue to write incoherent or incomplete sentences. By helping students understand that each sentence must stand alone just as a text message or status posting must stand alone, teachers can move students toward sentence coherence. The parts of speech can then be taught as a shared language and as a way to double-check their writing when they have the sense that something is missing or unclear.

Paragraph and Overall Coherence

Like the words within a sentence, sentences within a paragraph must relate to each other. Moreover, the sentences within a paragraph must build toward the main idea of that paragraph. To achieve this goal, students are typically taught that paragraphs need to have a topic sentence and that every sentence in that paragraph must be related to the topic sentence. When writing research papers, students may also be taught the convention that each paragraph must contain a "claim" (topic sentence), evidence (facts that support the claim), and interpretation (what the evidence reveals or means in relation to the larger question being explored in the paper). More advanced writers can be taught that the opening sentence of a paragraph should link the new paragraph to the preceding paragraph in some way and that the last sentence might provide a setup for the upcoming paragraph.

Paragraph coherence, and indeed coherence within the entire paper, may be a particular challenge for Generation 2.0. This is because they are used to a different way of making and understanding connections between texts. When sending text messages or writing status postings, context is typically understood. What this means is that the recipients of the message or the readers of the posting know the writer so well that they can fill in the information gaps. In fact, in many cases links between posts or texts are not expected because they exist in moments in time.

Transitions as a Tool for Identifying Connections between Ideas

This is not to say that youth do not have the ability to understand or create coherent texts. They just come about it differently. An examination of Web pages reveals that a well-designed Web page has an internal coherency. Everything on that page serves a particular purpose, even if that purpose is simply to demonstrate the wide and varied interests of a person. In order to introduce students to the idea of coherence and how one sentence must build on another, a teacher can lead students through the analysis of several Web pages.

Before tackling such a task, teachers should recognize that Web design includes the visual as well as the textual. Teachers do not have to gain an expertise in Web or graphic design, but they should understand the role color and design play in holding a Web page together. The different elements of a Web page matter, and there are, in fact, conventions that have developed over time. For instance, notice where navigation links and ads are placed. How does the page design lead the reader's eye? Most people read a Web page in an "F" pattern; they read the headline, then scan along the left side of the screen. Those elements on the far right and lower right tend to be ignored by most readers. Therefore, when considering page coherency, those elements that are placed in the "dead zone" often can be excluded from analysis.

In Web pages, pictures, illustrations, or graphics can serve to decorate, to augment the textual information, or to provide new information. The students and teacher can work together to identify how the Web page design links the graphic with the text. Is it done through a caption? Does the text refer to the picture? Does an image in the picture reflect or build on a textual description? Following Web page analysis, students can construct a rubric that identifies how elements within a Web page inform one another and what the reader needs to know in order to understand that website. Once the students identify those elements, students and teachers can work together to make parallels between Web page coherency and paragraph and essay coherency.

Teachers can help students realize the cognitive work they must do in order to understand the website and that in a traditional document, such as a paper, the writer helps the reader do the cognitive work because those visual clues are not available. Those aids, as discussed earlier in this chapter, include transitions and other connecting words.

Approaching the teaching of transitions inductively allows the student to understand the social purpose of words like transitions. The words are no longer just something that writers do, but serve to help the reader make sense of the student's ideas. The inductive approach is useful for every aspect of teaching the writer's craft. Although it does take longer to teach writing using this approach, with persistence the students not only comply with the writing requirements but begin to understand and internalize the reasons for different authorial moves.

Glossing to Check and Understand Coherence and Organization

Another strategy for working toward internal coherence within a paragraph and within the paper as a whole is the technique of glossing. Glossing is a long-standing method for supporting concept development in papers. With this technique, students are taught to read a paragraph and then recap or summarize it in a few words. However, rather than teaching glossing directly with the papers students are writing, it initially can be done with Web pages or Wikipedia entries.

If you are using a website, select a site of interest to students. The website should have multiple pages. Examine each page within the website and have students gloss (summarize) each page. This should demonstrate to the students that each page within a website serves a particular purpose. Then examine the glosses of each page and discuss how they work together to form a coherent website. This can be done several times with different websites. Students may discover that some websites are not coherent, and if so, that discovery can be used to discuss how the lack of coherency affects the effectiveness or quality of the site.

Students can also gloss Wikipedia entries and make corrections if they find an error or incoherent section of the entry. The act of glossing websites and Wikipedia entries not only teaches students how to gloss, it also teaches them to be more critical readers of online material. Actually fixing errors in a Wikipedia entry teaches them that they are participants in the world and can effect change, even if it is as little as clarifying a confusing sentence.

In traditional texts, the gloss can be used to demonstrate the overall organization of a piece of writing. When placed one after the other, the glosses from each paragraph create an outline. The students can then see how the author built his or her argument. This changes, however, when glossing is applied to a website. Rather than using the gloss to form an outline, the students can use a cluster chart to show the multiple connections between Web pages. Thus students will be able to deepen their understanding of how traditional texts differ from hypertexts while still forming a coherent whole.

Once students have the idea of glossing, they can use it to analyze their own writing, use it in peer conferencing, and use it to understand traditional texts they are reading. When glossing their own writing or using it in peer conferencing, if they find a paragraph difficult to gloss, it is likely that the paragraph has more than one central idea and thus does not meet the quality of coherence. Rather than telling the student that the paragraph is "wrong" or poorly written, the teacher or peer reviewer should ask questions such as "How is this idea connected to that idea?" or "Why did you choose that word?"

Such questions should lead the student to talking through his or her ideas and thus developing the ability to re-see what he or she is trying to say in the paper. The student then can select transitional words that adequately express what he or she is seeing as the connection between ideas, or the student might decide that a paragraph should be divided. If that happens, then the teacher can use genuine questions as a way to help the student determine how to expand each of those paragraphs in order to more fully explore the ideas within.

Although the approach described here is labor and time intensive, it pays off. Not only do students better understand the craft of writing, but they also become better readers and engage more with the content. If students are applying these revision techniques to the blog posts they wrote during the research phase of the project, they may also be less resistant to the revision process because they are not rewriting something they created once and thought they were done with. Hopefully, this approach will also contribute to greater student commitment to the writing project.

SUMMARY

Coherence refers to the way each element in a text relates to other elements and holds the entire text together. Organization is the act of ordering the text so that the reader is moved through a particular pattern of thinking.

Coherence exists at the sentence level, the paragraph level, and the level of the whole paper. It is created through the author's use of rhetorical tools such as transitions. Organization also exists within paragraphs and at the holistic level. Organization is dictated by the genre and expectations of the intended audience. Coherence and organization are important because they help the reader make sense of the text.

Members of Generation 2.0 may struggle with creating organized and coherent texts because they are used to online exchanges that are dependent on the reader's contextual knowledge or the timeliness of the posting. Hyperlinks also change the nature of coherency and organization. Coherency and organization on a Web page are constructed by the designer's use of hyperlinks; however, once a reader leaves a website, the designer is no longer in control. Generation 2.0 is sensitive to coherence through their ability to follow narratives and ideas across multiple modalities. They know how texts refer to one another through the repetition of images, music, or central characters.

Several different types of lessons can be used to support Generation 2.0 in the quest to learn how to write coherent and organized traditional papers. Instant messages and status postings can be examined to develop an understanding of what makes a complete idea. Unclear sentences can be presented in instant message or status posting form in order to consider what additional information is needed to make the idea clear. Once students have an understanding of what makes a complete clause, they can be taught the art of sentence combining. They can also apply the paramedic method to long, unclear sentences.

Paragraph coherence can be taught by first examining Web pages to understand how each Web page holds together. Elements of page design can be paralleled to transitions and other rhetorical cues people use to create paragraph coherency. Glossing of Web pages, websites, texts students read, and student texts can be used to teach paragraph coherency, as well as overall coherency and organization.

Although the techniques discussed in this chapter are labor and time intensive, it is suggested that these methods will result in increased student learning of the content as well as improved online and offline reading and writing skills. Student motivation may also increase since they will have a lower frustration level and an increased commitment to the writing project.

Chapter Nine

Word Choice and Spelling

In this chapter, we turn our attention to word choice and spelling. Although these elements of writing are often left to last as part of the editing process, they are important in that each contributes to the meaning being imparted by the text, as well as the relationship of the writer to the intended audience. Despite claims in the popular press to the contrary, Generation 2.0 has a sense of language use and understands concepts of spelling.

WORD CHOICE

As students work on building their paper by seeking connections within the material they collected, they can also be attending to their word choice. The words we use when writing serve multiple functions. Our words capture concepts and show relationships between concepts. The vocabulary we use also contributes to the creation of voice and persona. Too often, perhaps as the result of learning vocabulary through exercises rather than for genuine purposes of making meaning, students think of vocabulary as a way to give the teacher what he or she wants or to show what they know, rather than as a way to say what they want more precisely. However, outside of school, youth demonstrate a love for and understanding of words through their play with words in online exchanges or in the raps and rhymes they create.

Discussion of word choice and language use occurs less frequently when people consider the implications of the new literacies on student writing than do issues such as spelling and grammar; however, when teaching and assessing writing, teachers do pay attention to language use. For instance, word choice is one of the traits in the well-known 6 + 1 Writing Traits program. State exams, such as the one administered in New York, include language use as one of the elements on the scoring rubric. As such, the use of simplistic language or the misuse of words can result in student writing being penalized. Even worse, the writer's intention may be misunderstood.

There are countless books and lesson plans available for teaching vocabulary. What must be remembered, however, is that word choice is not arbitrary but is tied to the intention of the author and who the intended audience is. Intention includes not only what the author wants to say, but also the image that the author wants to project. As such, simply teaching new words will not move a student toward increasing his or her use of new vocabulary. There must be a need for the word before the word is used.

The use of computers for composition may have contributed to the introduction of unintended language into a piece of student-created text. Specifically, dependence on the spell checker or thesaurus function of a word processor can lead to students using words that do not accurately convey what they are trying to say. This phenomenon may be related to a student's trusting the computer software over his or her own knowledge, the student wanting to please the teacher through the use of what the student thinks is advanced vocabulary, the student wanting to portray himself or herself as being smart—or it may be due to the fact that the student is uninvested in the assignment and simply selects the first choice offered by the software. Determining the reason for word choice should be discovered through conversation with the student. The simple question "Why did you pick that word?" can open up a world of understanding.

What should be avoided is making a judgment that the student doesn't understand the importance of word choice in text production. When we think about it from the perspective of youth engagement in the new literacies, it is clear that youth do in fact pay attention to word choice when what they are writing matters to them.

For instance, Joaquín paid close attention to the words he used in his raps. They not only had to meet meter and rhyme patterns, but he was highly aware of how his word choice was part of his public persona. As he said, he refused to use profanity because he wanted to respect the words and represent himself in a certain way. Joaquín's attention to language was also apparent in his speech—he would often check with his English-speaking listener as to whether the word he used was the correct one when he was trying to explain something.

Lisa was also sensitive to word choice. Lisa said that she could tell when her friends were being serious by the care that was taken in each post, and care was shown through word choice as well as more precise spelling. Youth also report that they are sensitive to who is on the receiving end of their messages when they send messages. When they are sending a message to someone with whom they do not have a closer relationship, in addition to making sure that their messages are error free, they also tend to pay more attention to their vocabulary choices.

VOCABULARY INSTRUCTION

One way to approach vocabulary instruction is by using the spell check and thesaurus functions of a word processor. When a word processor marks a word as wrong, students can be taught to examine each of the suggested words and to consider which word best matches what they intended. If they are unfamiliar with any of the suggested words, they can use the built-in dictionary or an online dictionary to look up the suggested words. They can use a graphic organizer to build a representation of words they find promising.

Students can also be taught to use the "find" function to seek out words they use frequently. Once they identify how often they use a particular word, they can be encouraged to use the thesaurus function to find replacement words. However, they should be taught to use restraint with the thesaurus and to use it in conjunction with a dictionary so that they select the word that best represents their intended meaning and best fits with the needs of their audience. Too often students trust the software rather than themselves and choose words that are not necessarily best for the text.

As Joaquín shows us, youth may also have a sense of vocabulary and word choice through their experiences with writing raps, fanfiction, and song lyrics. Texting and status posting on social networking sites also encourage word play, which can be drawn on when writing. Youth who create video remixes and anime remixes or who construct social network pages filled with songs and images know how important it is to pick just the right graphic or video clip or song to capture how they want to represent themselves. This acute awareness of the importance of the "just right" image or song can be used as a springboard for discussion about word choice.

Simple questions can also be used to trigger students' thinking about word choice. Rather than telling students that a particular phrasing is awkward or does not make sense, ask the student "Why did you choose this word?" or "What did you mean here?" Listen carefully to the student's explanation and point out when the student uses clearer language. If a teacher understands that ambiguous word choices or misused words serve as placeholders as the student struggles to understand for himself or herself what he or she is trying to say, then helping the student think through the idea through straightforward questions is more helpful than simply pointing out errors.

A tool that can help teachers learn to ask questions and allow students to think out loud is to take notes as the student talks. The teacher can scribe what the student is saying, jot it down in chart form, or even place it in a rough outline. The note form depends on what the student is thinking about. Taking the position of note taker will help the teacher refrain from dominating the conversation. The teacher can also leave the notes with the student, which the student can then use to help revise the draft. Coincidentally, the note taking also serves as modeling for students when they peer conference.

The goal is to teach students to trust themselves as thinkers and writers rather than trusting an expert, whether that expert is the computer software or the teacher. Of course, students may resist these lessons. They may want to hand over responsibility or they may not be invested enough in the assignment to take the time to consider word choice. Those issues, however, are not the fault of spell checking or technology in general but need to be addressed through curriculum. By appealing to the idea of a real audience and real purposes (even if that real audience is an anonymous test reader and the purpose is to pass a test), a teacher can begin tapping into the knowledge youth have about audience, purpose, and the power of words.

SPELLING DEVELOPMENT

Once the paper is built and revised enough to ensure solid organization and coherency within sentences, paragraphs, and the paper as a whole, the final step is editing. At this point we can turn our attention to smoothing out errors in spelling, grammar, and punctuation. It is important to remember that although these may seem like surface issues that can be attended to at the last moment, it is these items that most people notice first and that have the greatest impact on how the writer is perceived by the reader. Even if a piece of writing is well organized and contains a compelling argument, if the text contains multiple errors, even surface errors that do not change the deeper meaning of the text, the authority of the writer is undermined and respect for the text is lost. This is especially true in test-taking situations or where readers perceive themselves as being of a higher social rank than the writer.

Spelling

Spelling, or rather nonstandard spelling and language use, is one of the first concerns that come up when people discuss youth use of digital technologies. Youth use of instant messaging and texting is seen as the major culprit. Here we explore the common beliefs about youth and spelling conventions. Lisa's experience is used to illustrate some of the concerns and realities of the issues. Remember, Lisa serves to clarify the different aspects of spelling and youth engagement with digital technologies, but she is not meant to represent all youth. This chapter includes suggestions for ways to use the concept of participatory culture and youth engagement in the new literacies to support student development of conventional spelling in school-based writing.

Before we begin, let us briefly review the nature of English spelling. Even though it may seem to be incomprehensible at times, the reality is that the English spelling system is not arbitrary. There is actually a great deal of information hidden within what appears to be a sometimes capricious mix of letters. Specifically, English spelling maintains the history of a word, helps us understand meaning, and also helps us translate the word into sound.

For example, the words *cow* and *beef* both refer to the same animal, but *cow* is descended from the Germanic word *kuh* and *beef* is from the French *boeuf*. The two different words make clear that one is the animal in the field and the other is the animal prepared for dinner. The two words also carry the history of the Norman occupation of England and the relationship of the English to the French. Furthermore, the spellings of the words help us translate the word into sound through our knowledge of sound-letter correspondence. We learn that the letter *c* followed by an *a* or *o* represents the /k/ sound. We also learn that two vowels together represent the long sound of the first vowel, as in the /e/ of *beef*.

Meaning is also carried in the spellings of words. This is apparent in homophones, those words that have the same sound but different spellings and different meanings. These are words such as *through* and *threw* or *see* and *sea*. If the word is spoken by itself without any context, it is not clear what meaning is intended, but when written, the reader immediately knows the intended meaning based on the spelling, even if the word is presented in isolation.

Because the spelling of words imparts meaning, it is important to pay attention to both how words are encoded (written) and decoded (read). Decoding essentially means translating the written symbols into spoken form. Research tells us that there are four different ways to read words. One way is that we apply grapheme (letter) knowledge to phoneme (sound) knowledge. That is what is typically meant when teachers ask students "What sound does this letter make?" Strictly speaking, letters do not make sounds—they represent sounds given their relationship to other letters in the word or sentence—but nonetheless, at the most basic level, we use our knowledge of sound-letter correspondence to decode a word. Once we speak the new word, we are able to tap into our knowledge of oral language to recognize the word.

A second way that we recognize words is by sight. Sight words are typically thought of as those words that have irregular spellings, thus making it difficult (if not impossible) to decode using phonics. However, research also tells us that once we have decoded a word, pronounced it, and mapped it to our knowledge of what that word means, then we no longer have to decode the word each time we see it and instead recognize it by sight. This on-sight recognition moves us toward automaticity in reading.

A third way of reading involves using predictions based on the context of the sentence. To accomplish this task, we use what we know about the situation described in the sentence, an aspect of the word, and then predict what the word is going to be. So in a sentence like "She had bacon and e____ for breakfast," a child who is familiar with that meal would predict that the missing word is *eggs*, based on the other words in the sentence as well as the letter *e*. A child who has no knowledge of a bacon-and-egg breakfast might struggle to complete the sentence.

The fourth way to read a word is by seeing how similar it is to other known words. This strategy tends to be used by more experienced readers and writers. When drawing on this strategy, readers and writers look for rhyming patterns and visual letter patterns, and they use their knowledge of grammar to make guesses about the word (such as the use of the *-ed* ending).

The four principles discussed above deal mostly with the act of decoding or reading and comprehension. But what about encoding or writing? A child's development of spelling is seen as moving through stages. Young children first engage in scribbles, then draw on phonetic strategies (matching sounds to letters), then transition to more standard spellings. In the third or transitional stage, children depend less on phonetic knowledge and more on visual strategies (such as analogies and memory of known words). The final stage of spelling development is the standard stage, where we use what is recognized as the "right" way to spell each word.

It is becoming clearer that children do not move through these stages in a neat progression but rather draw on strategies associated with each stage at any given time depending on the task at hand. Thus when writing, a child may copy some words, draw on memory for others, use phonetic strategies for some, and turn to visual strategies and analogies for yet other words. These principles and stages of reading and spelling are most often applied to young children. Preteens and teens are thought to have reached the standard stage in spelling, yet they will continue to draw on these different strategies while composing. The fear of teachers and other adults is that youths' mastery of standard spelling is being damaged by their use of nonstandard digital forms. The research, however, indicates that this fear is unfounded.

SPELLING IN THE TWENTY-FIRST CENTURY

What can we learn from Lisa's experience as someone who struggled with spelling yet seemed able to move past that struggle and even integrate conventional spelling into instant messaging—a place most people associate with nonstandard spelling?

First, it is important to think about spelling within the grand scheme of writing. Spelling is considered a surface error in writing instruction. Minor spelling errors typically do not affect the deeper meaning of a text. As long as the reader has a sense of what the author is trying to say, even errors that deviate significantly from accepted spelling generally do not change overall meaning.

Nonetheless, youth use of nonstandard spelling in writing seems to cause angst among teachers and other adults. Newspaper interviews with teachers and parents reveal attitudes that the use of abbreviations and nonstandard spellings associated with instant messaging and texting is rude, sloppy, undisciplined, careless, shocking, inappropriate, shoddy, alarming, and represents the death of editing. Youth, however, indicate that they are aware of their use of nonstandard spellings but sometimes slip into using those spellings when doing writing for school if they are rushed or unengaged in the writing assignment. When written communication has a serious purpose, youth pay more attention to their writing.

For example, during lighthearted exchanges using instant messaging, Lisa would rapidly type out responses that were sprinkled with misspellings and typographic errors that she would sometimes fix but often ignore. However, she and her friends would slow down, correct typographic and spelling errors, and deliberately choose their words when involved in a serious online conversation.

Although misspellings represent surface errors, those errors are windows into what youth know about language as well as their sense of whom they are writing to and the tone and voice they wish their writing to carry. First, according to researchers at the University of Coventry in the United Kingdom, youth use of nonstandard spellings demonstrates the user's phonemic knowledge (Plester, Wood, & Joshi, 2009). If youth were not aware of the sounds within language, they would not be able to map letters and numbers in place of standard words (such as "l8r" for "later").

Second, youth often comment about how awkward the online writing of adults is. The youth note that the adults' careful attention to grammar, spelling, and mechanics demonstrates that the adults do not understand that instant messaging and texting represent spontaneous conversation rather than carefully thought-out discourse. Other youth, however, note that it is strange when adults use the conventions associated with texting because those are practices associated with youth. Such comments show us that youth are sensitive to how language is used across different groups of people and what fits and does not fit with particular group identities (such as teens and adults).

Given the two different insights into the nature of spelling in the twenty-first century, it is clear that the problem is not that members of Generation 2.0

do not know how to spell or edit, or even their lack of attention to spelling or editing. Instead, the problem may be multifold. First, youth may not be given the time necessary to carefully craft the writing they are doing for school (as in on-demand writing), and thus they may revert to the well-honed skills developed through the quick writing required for texting and instant messaging. Second, youth may not have a clear idea of who their audience is or what their purpose is for writing a particular piece. This problem also leads to the issue of engagement. If the student does not know whom they are writing for or why they are writing (beyond its being a school assignment), they are less likely to pay attention to their writing.

When youth know their audience, they pay attention to what they write. As Lisa showed, she would edit her instant messages especially when the messages where of a serious nature. The lack of engagement may in fact contribute to the lack of interest in editing. Therefore, it is not that texting or instant messaging is causing the "death of editing," but rather the lack of compelling reasons to edit. Finally, a youth may have the time, may have the interest, but may not have the understanding of the demands of the genre or the intended audience of the piece. This final aspect is the one teachers are most apt to address in formal lessons, but it appears to be the one youth already have a sense of.

Spelling Instruction

Spelling errors can come about for a number of reasons, including a student's heavy use of phonics rules, typographic errors, or confusing one word with another. The use of the spell checker and automatic correction within a word processor ostensibly should help address many spelling difficulties, but often students become dependent on spell check or overly trust spell check. As a result, students may either fail to proofread their writing, or they may take the suggestion of the spell checker over their own knowledge.

When this occurs, we often find the appearance of words that are not what the student intended and do not fit the sentence. Often these are homophones and homonyms (such as *to/too/two* or *new/knew*), or students might use the wrong word such as "impotence" instead of "importance." This has been a long-standing issue and has been tackled through the humorous spell-checker poem written by Jerrold Zar in 1992. Teachers often use this poem to stress the importance of proofreading. A more recent (and ribald) performance of Taylor Mali's poem "The the impotence of proofreading" on YouTube also speaks to this problem.

There are many ideas available online and in numerous books for teaching and reinforcing the importance of proofreading. However, existing materials often fail to address why a word is misspelled. One approach to addressing the problems brought about by students' overdependence on spell checker is to teach how the software actually works. Students can be taught how a spell checker operates, simply by comparing the words typed against an internal dictionary. When the typed word does not match something in the dictionary, it is marked as an error. The software then identifies possible intended words using an algorithm that examines the letter combinations of the attempted word and compares those combinations to words in the dictionary. The computer program does not have the intelligence to consider meaning.

This idea can be made concrete by having students actually explore the contents of the spell checker dictionary by testing a variety of words and spellings and by adding specialized words that are not in the dictionary (such as science terms) to the database. For instance, students can analyze a list of words, some correct, some incorrect, some in the dictionary, some not, and some in British spelling rather than American spelling. They can type each word into a document to test how the spell checker responds. The teacher and students can discuss why the program responds as it does and what the writer's actions should be in response to the spell checker. These activities can appeal to the students' sense of play, their enjoyment of experimentation, and ultimately can help the students see that the spell checker and thesaurus are not infallible tools but simply an extension of the quite fallible human mind.

SUMMARY

Attention to word choice and spelling are often left to the last phase of the writing process. However, these elements of composition are important aspects of meaning. Attention to word choice while writing should be taught as a way of making connections between ideas, precisely capturing concepts, and creating authorial voice. Spelling should be taught as a way of understanding how language works. Examinations of technology such as the spell checker and thesaurus can be used to support student understandings of attention to word choice and spelling. Youth engagement in writing raps, rhymes, and short messages can also be used to build student awareness of word choice and spelling variations. Rather than seeing youth engagement in digital technologies as detrimental, teachers can use the skills youth have as a starting point for exploration into language.

Chapter Ten

Punctuation

This chapter is not intended to provide a comprehensive lesson in punctuation use. There are books upon books that do so in many different ways and with different levels of effectiveness depending upon the knowledge and needs of the reader. The purpose here is to point out that punctuation use is not about following rules but rather about making meaning. If a writer does not use accepted conventions, he or she increases the risk of being misunderstood.

There are five straightforward punctuation marks, and most children master them early in their education. The period (.) indicates the end of a sentence, and as discussed earlier, a sentence at minimum contains a subject (who) and a predicate (did what). The question mark (?), which is sometimes called the interrogation or query, indicates that the sentence is a question, and the exclamation point (!) is used to show surprise or high emotion. Quotation marks (" ") show words spoken by someone or words taken from another text, and parentheses are used when there is a need to insert something into the text that is nonessential but helpful.

More difficult and less common punctuation marks include the colon (:), which indicates a transition point in the sentence; the semicolon (;), which separates independent clauses or statements while indicating that those clauses have a close relationship; and the dash (—), which shows abruptness or irregularity between ideas in a sentence. Many well-educated adults struggle with the correct use of these forms of punctuation, and they are less frequently seen in writing, whether online or in traditional texts.

The two most common, but also most commonly misused, punctuation marks are the comma (,) and the apostrophe ('). The apostrophe is used for contractions (turning "do not" into "don't"). In contractions, the apostrophe takes the place of the missing letter or letters. The apostrophe is also used to mark ownership (possessive case) such as "my mother's house." The confusion between "its" (indicating possession) and "it's" (the contraction of "it is") is of course one of the exceptions to this rule.

The comma also has multiple uses. It is used to mark a series, as in "People often make mistakes when using commas, apostrophes, colons, and semicolons." Commas also separate clauses and phrases. When the comma separates independent clauses, a coordinating conjunction must be used as well; otherwise the writer will have written what is called a "comma splice" ("The comma is the most common punctuation mark, it is the most frequently misused punctuation mark as well."), which is a type of run-on sentence. The following sentence is correct: "The comma is the most common punctuation mark, and it is the most frequently misused punctuation mark as well." Both these clauses could function alone as sentences, but the comma combined with the conjunction shows a relationship between the two ideas.

Commas also serve to separate dependent clauses and appositives from the main clause of a sentence. A dependent clause is a phrase that cannot stand on its own as a sentence. For example, "Although the comma is a confusing punctuation mark, we need it to keep meaning clear." In this case the section before the comma is the dependent clause. The word "although" makes the clause dependent on something else. If the second part of the sentence were missing, we would be left asking "Although what?" The second half of the sentence is an independent clause because it has a subject ("we") and a predicate ("need it to keep meaning clear"). It makes sense by itself—although the pronoun "it" would need to be replaced by a specific noun in order to be fully understandable.

An appositive is a phrase that provides additional information about the subject of a sentence but can be removed without changing the relationship of the subject to the predicate. For example, "The comma, the most commonly used punctuation mark, is the most commonly misused punctuation mark." If we remove the appositive phrase "the most commonly used punctuation mark" the sentence reads "The comma is the most commonly misused punctuation mark." The sentence still carries the intended meaning.

The purposes of the different punctuation marks, as described above, represent a cultural agreement. However, language is constantly changing as a result of people moving from one place to another and coming together with people who speak differently. New inventions also give rise to new words. Similarly, punctuation changes over time. In fact, of all the conventions of writing, punctuation is probably the most sensitive to change.

In the 1600s, punctuation was used to indicate pauses during speech. A comma indicated a pause of one count, and a period indicated a pause of four counts. An examination of written materials from the early 1800s shows that punctuation was unpredictable at that time. Even the U.S. Constitution shows the variability of punctuation use at the time. Specifically, different copies of the Second Amendment (the right to bear arms) show commas placed differently. The official version of the amendment has three commas, but some states ratified versions with only two commas.

Now, however, punctuation use is more codified. It is understood to be important because it carries meaning-making responsibilities and is used for specific purposes. The ability to follow the sometimes confusing rules of punctuation also identifies the writer as someone who is either well educated (either formally or self-taught) or highly aware of the art of writing.

The changing nature of punctuation continues today and is perhaps increasing or at least more apparent due to digital technologies. Naomi Baron (2008), a linguist at American University, argues that part of the issue is that the online world uses punctuation differently than the ink-and-paper world. For instance, punctuation and spaces are not used in URLs, and people are learning how to read those forms. As a result, people may be paying less attention to punctuation, resulting in what Baron calls a "whatever" approach to writing. That is, punctuation is unimportant as long as we are able to accomplish our purposes. Baron also tells us that her students say they do not type in apostrophes when writing papers because they assume the autocorrect function of their word-processing program will correct it. Youth not only are seeing fewer uses of punctuation, they are also finding less need to use it themselves.

However, people still use punctuation, but do so with an eye toward functionality. Baron looked closely at the use of punctuation in instant messaging and texting and found her participants left off ending periods except when more than one sentence appeared in a message. In those cases, the period was used to mark the different sentences. Although Baron does not discuss this possibility, it may be that periods are not used at the end of single-sentence messages because the sender and receiver know it is the end of the utterance. Clicking <enter> or <send> or pressing the "return" key may serve the same function as a period.

Naomi Baron also found that apostrophes tend not to be used and suggests that this may be because it is more complex to input an apostrophe into a cell phone message. However, Lauren Squires (2007), a student of Baron, analyzed the differences in apostrophe use between men and women and found that women typically use apostrophes more than men when sending instant messages. She suggests that this might be because women are more sensitive to who is in power and they recognize that adherence to standard forms helps make a good impression on the reader. According to Squires, the end result is that women tend to follow more standard uses of language in writing than men. It is unclear where these changes will take us. It may be that eventually the apostrophe will fall into disuse and "your" will replace "you're." Widely used languages tend toward regularity over time. Until then, punctuation remains a challenge for the teacher of Generation 2.0.

For now, variability in punctuation use is a visible representation of the tensions between the changing nature of language, apparent in the online world of texting and status postings, and the static nature of academic English used in formal papers written for publication or grades. So where does that leave teachers and the need to support students in learning the standard conventions that still carry weight in today's world?

ADDRESSING THE CHALLENGE OF PUNCTUATION THROUGH IMAGE MAINTENANCE

When members of Generation 2.0 are online they are building digital portfolios or dossiers that construct a perspective on who they are and who they want to be. It is for that reason that issues of privacy have recently become so important to youth. Whereas the Internet used to be considered a place where an individual could be anonymous, now the Internet is understood to be a place where information can (and does) easily escape an individual's control. Thus, maintaining what information is online is growing in importance.

A 2010 study by the Pew Internet and American Life project showed that Generation 2.0 is actually more sensitive to issues of privacy and more apt to take action to restrict access to their information than millenials or older people (Madden & Smith, 2010). The growing awareness of privacy issues was also evident in the uproar that occurred in early 2010 when Facebook created what many considered to be an overly complex process for protecting one's privacy. Many people threatened to leave Facebook rather than risk having their privacy imperiled. Facebook eventually responded by adjusting its privacy settings, and a mass exodus from Facebook was avoided. Members of Generation 2.0, however, are growing in their awareness that they, or their information, are, in fact, the product being sold to advertisers whenever they post something online.

With this in mind, we have the sense that Generation 2.0 knows that they are constantly "on stage" or under scrutiny because of digital technology. They spend large chunks of time maintaining their online image by adding to and deleting content pertaining to them. As such, teachers can use Generation 2.0's awareness of public perception as well as authentic writing opportunities to build motivation to use standard conventions.

First, students and the teacher can examine a variety of texts including websites and discuss what their perception of the writer is based on how the author uses language and conventional spelling, grammar, and punctuation. Attention should also be paid to genre and textual modes, in that different modes and genres require different levels of formality in writing and some forms even demand nonstandard language and convention use.

For instance, in texting and instant messaging, the use of capitalization and punctuation is considered overly correct and indicates that the response is possibly contrived or less spontaneous than is desirable. This convention arose because instant messaging and texting are considered more akin to speech than to writing. The teacher and students should also explore fan-fiction sites, e-zine sites, or whatever other websites and texts the students regularly visit to notice the stylistic nuances and to understand how the use of different conventions sends different messages to the reader.

The intended audience also makes a difference. Students and teacher can discuss how an e-mail sent to someone who is in a socially higher position (such as an employer, teacher, or college professor) should follow stricter use of spelling, grammar, and punctuation conventions than an e-mail to a friend. In this conversation, students may note that they rarely use e-mail to commu-nicate with friends, a statement that can lead to a discussion of how different modes of communication are used for different purposes. For instance, status postings and texts are used for communication between friends and thus are expected to contain less use of standard conventions in order to send the mes-sage of informality and trust.

On the other hand, e-mails tend to be used for more official communica-tions, and word-processed letters are the most formal of communications and thus require the most attention to conventions. Websites and wikis created for a community of fans of a celebrity will be less formal than a website cre-ated to represent a company. For instance, a person trying to market crafts on Etsy.com, a website that independent artists use for marketing their products, should pay attention to grammar, spelling, and punctuation because he or she wants to give the impression of being a responsible entrepreneur who will respond to the needs of the client.

Finally, discussing the intended audience of research papers (or any school-based piece of writing) and how members of that audience will perceive the student writer will move the students toward understanding the nature of academic writing alongside all the other types of text production they engage in. Moving through this process will not necessarily result in huge improve-ments in student use of standard conventions or even in their understanding of the different conventions; direct instruction on the various ways in which punctuation should be used in academic writing is still necessary.

However, allowing students the time to explore and deduce the meaning of punctuation will result in greater motivation and less resistance to learning and using standard punctuation. Furthermore, this process will recognize and legitimize the conventions the students already know and use from their everyday life, rather than sending the message that what they do is "wrong."

SUMMARY

Punctuation is an important aspect of writing because it helps make meaning clear. Each punctuation mark carries a specific purpose, and some punctuation marks, such as the comma and the apostrophe, have multiple purposes. The comma and the apostrophe are also the most commonly misused and misunderstood punctuation marks.

Part of the difficulty with punctuation is that it is the most sensitive to change. At one time punctuation was used to show pauses in speech. Since the eighteenth century, punctuation use has become more standardized. However, the development of digital communication tools such as instant messaging and social networking shows continued change in punctuation use. Research indicates that the apostrophe is becoming less commonly used for contractions, and other punctuation marks are excluded from the online world of URLs. Along with the changes brought by digital technology, attitudes are shifting as well, and some people are taking a more relaxed attitude toward punctuation use. Punctuation is not going away, however. People continue to use punctuation when the function is important and when they want to gain respect from their readers.

Teachers can address the challenge of teaching punctuation by appealing to Generation 2.0's sense of image maintenance. Members of Generation 2.0 know that what they post online is seen by many people. They also know that once something is posted online it may move out of their control. Members of Generation 2.0 thus think about what they post and what they remove from the Internet. How writers use punctuation can be taught as part of the image a writer constructs when creating a text.

The importance of genre and mode should also be considered when teaching punctuation. Each genre and mode has its own set of conventions regarding punctuation. Audience and purpose must also be considered when discussing conventions. Direct instruction in the conventions of punctuation may still be needed, but allowing students the time to explore and deduce the meaning of punctuation will contribute to greater motivation and interest in spending time on text production.

Chapter Eleven

What Next?

As teachers know, many young people have built strong skills in the new literacies but continue to struggle with school literacies. While some people may argue that school literacies are passé, it remains a fact that facility in academic reading and writing is seen as a marker of success in most countries and communities. However, skill in school literacies is not enough. Therefore, the purpose of this book is to help teachers deepen their understanding of who their students are and how to use the qualities of Generation 2.0 to help build students' writing skills as well as the ways of thinking that are part of the twenty-first-century information economy.

Young people need to know how to negotiate the world of Web 2.0 as well as how to be successful with school-based literacies. Those youth who have limited access to Web 2.0 technologies are as much at risk for marginalization as those who struggle in school. This book attempts to acknowledge and honor the wealth of literacies young people develop outside of school while building their facility in school-based literacies. It is hoped that young people who are comfortable in both worlds can then use that knowledge to create a better life for themselves and their families and to contribute to a more just and humane society.

The intent of this book is also to help teachers think about their own teaching practice, especially in respect to technology integration. It is hoped that the reader will take what has been presented here and will transform it into practice that makes sense for the individual teaching situation. Therefore, this final chapter provides some ways that teachers can develop their own approaches to teaching writing to Generation 2.0.

UNDERSTAND YOUR OWN LITERACIES

Take some time to think about your own literacies. Keep a literacy log for a few days and make note of every interaction you have with text. Notice whether your text use is related to school, work, or pleasure. Remember to keep your definition of what a text is expansive. Texting, status posting, and reading a website or blog are as much literacy activities as reading a novel. Ask yourself the following questions. Use the answers to think about who you are as a literate person and what your literacies mean to you.

1. What literacies do you find to be the most essential to your well-being, whether you enjoy them or not?
2. Why are they so essential?
3. Which literacies bring you the most joy?
4. What is pleasurable about them?
5. Where do you feel a sense of play, exploration, experimentation, and collaboration?
6. How does all this help connect you to people and issues you care about?

Also pay attention to the technologies you engage with on a regular basis.
7. Why are the technologies you use important to you?
8. What do they help you do that you would not be able to do if you did not have those technologies?
9. Think about how you learned those literacies and those technologies. How do those technologies connect you to your friends, family, and community?

GETTING TO KNOW YOUR STUDENTS

The best teachers know their students. The best teachers also know we should never assume anything about the background of a student based on appearance, family history, neighborhood of origin, race or ethnicity, gender, religion, and so on. Each student is an individual with a unique set of life circumstances. At the same time, however, each student and that student's family are part of a community and cultural group, so as we get to know the individual student we also need to increase our understanding of the student's family, community, and cultural history.

A student's technological history is also part of that background. As the year begins, teachers should ask direct questions about students' experiences with the new literacies. Beginning-of-the-year questionnaires are useful, and one is included in this book. But teachers should also just listen as students talk to each other. Listening is especially important because often people are not consciously aware of their numerous literacy practices or they may not consider the things they do worth mentioning. For instance, Lisa and her friends did not consider instant messaging to be writing. It was, for them, another form of talk. Yet, as they exchanged instant messages they were involved in a significant literacy practice and participating in a vibrant communicative community.

Judge Not

As someone who is a member of a different generation from the students, we may find it tempting to judge students' involvement in various literacy practices. Teachers tend to be people who did well in school and who learned and followed the rules of school. Teachers also often are those who learned best through traditional teaching methods such as lectures and note taking. However, most students are not going to be teachers and thus need a different approach to learning.

The different learning needs of students are further complicated by the world of Web 2.0 and participatory culture. Recognizing that most students are not going to be excited or motivated by the same things as you is important. Suspending judgment when listening to youth discuss those things that do motivate them is equally important. When listening to a member of Generation 2.0 discuss his or her success in a role-playing game, set aside any temptation to dismiss this involvement as being "just play" or "a waste of time." Be genuinely interested in the activity and ask honest questions about the student's involvement in the game. As you listen to the answers, ask yourself the following types of questions.

1. What type of thinking is this student engaging in?
2. What literacies is the student drawing on as he or she games?
3. What type of person is this student constructing himself or herself to be?
4. What is it about this activity that excites and motivates the student?

Seeking to answer these types of questions will help you understand and consequently reach the student more effectively than dismissing the activity as unimportant for learning.

After you have a sense of your own literacy and technology practices as well as your students', take some time to compare and contrast your literacies to theirs. Here are some questions and ideas to consider.

1. What do the two of you share that you can build on in the classroom?
2. What do the students know that you can benefit from learning about?

3. What do you have to offer the students?
4. Look beyond the school-based literacies to those that are part of the communities you are both members of.
5. Remember, the issue is not how to use each piece of technology (although you and the students can learn about those from each other); the most important issue is how the new literacies allow people to build a different relationship to information, to other people, and to participate in the world in new ways.

CONSTRUCTING THE NEW LITERACIES CLASSROOM

What should the new literacies classroom be like? There are no easy or straightforward answers to that question beyond "It all depends." It all depends on who you are, who your students are, what the community is like, and most importantly, what your goals and objectives are. Therefore, once teachers understand their practices and the literacy and technology knowledge of their students, it is imperative that they carefully consider their goals and objectives before designing lessons and assignments that draw on the new literacies.

Without careful consideration of what he or she hopes to accomplish, the teacher risks falling into the trap of simply adding technology to old ways of thinking. Colin Lankshear and Michele Knobel (2008) call this the "old wine in new bottles" syndrome, or the repackaging of the same content in a fancy new container. For instance, simply assigning students to blog instead of writing in journals is a form of old wine/new bottles. Such an assignment does not make blogging any different from paper-and-ink technology.

Conversely, having students blog responses to real issues, include links to current texts (including audio, video, and graphics), and comment on other blogs creates something new and engages students in new types of thinking. However, to move the students to this new form of writing requires careful forethought on the part of the teacher, trust in the process, and the willingness to let go of some of the control of the online interaction. It also requires explicit instruction around the norms and purposes of blogging for those students who are new to the medium. Adding technology without rethinking the purpose of the technology is insufficient if we wish to tap into the new literacies and the ways of thinking supported by the new literacies.

DESIGNING NEW LITERACIES LEARNING OBJECTIVES

To avoid this pitfall, we need to consider just what it is we want our students to be doing. However, new literacies learning objectives are more than the type of objectives generally associated with lesson planning. Whereas a traditional learning objective identifies a particular behavior or understanding the teacher is aiming to develop in students, a new literacies objective identifies the type of participation or way of thinking that is the desired outcome. For example, a traditional learning objective might be "After completing the lesson on simple sentence combining, students will be able to combine simple sentences into compound sentences using the correct coordinating conjunction and punctuation."

In traditional learning objectives, the outcome must be observable, and in *behavioral* learning objectives the outcome must be measurable, so the criterion of "with a 90 percent accuracy rate" would be added to the objective. Such objectives allow the teacher to see whether the student was able to combine the sentences, use a conjunction that demonstrated the relationship of the two clauses, and use the correct punctuation as determined by standard academic English. The criterion or measurement also allows the teacher to determine whether the student is able to reliably complete the task over a number of trials. By requiring a high enough rate of success, the teacher can assume that the student has a grasp of the task.

Having written such a learning objective, the teacher now knows that he or she must create a lesson that teaches coordinating conjunctions and the use of the comma. The teacher can then assess student learning either by having the students complete a test or worksheet requiring them to combine sentences, or for a bit more authentic assessment, by having the students identify the simple sentences in their own writing and then combining those sentences. Of course, doing the latter would actually require an additional lesson and objective, which might be "After completing a lesson in simple sentence structure, students will be able to identify simple sentences in their own writing with a 90 percent accuracy rate." Then the second lesson on sentence combining would follow.

These types of learning objectives serve to support discrete tasks but are insufficient to address the complexities of the new literacies and participatory culture. Therefore, a new type of objective is required. Let us start by returning to the skills Jenkins identified as being learned through membership in a participatory culture.

1. Experimentation as a way to solve problems.
2. Learning from simulations.
3. Collaboration.
4. Drawing on multiple tools to develop knowledge.
5. Knowing how to judge various sources of information.
6. Adjusting one's way of interacting based on the community in which one is operating.

7. Following a narrative across multiple modalities.
8. Performing different roles or identities based on the requirements of the context.
9. Drawing from a variety of sources to create something new.
10. Multitasking.
11. Searching for, synthesizing, and disseminating information.

With those skills in mind, a new literacies learning objective might be "After the lesson on defining the qualities of a good blog, students will be able to identify and link to blogs that connect them to an online community through which they can learn about an area of interest."

This objective serves to allow students to experiment by looking at a range of blogs and testing them against the criteria that were determined collaboratively. They are judging various sources of information, adjusting what they link to based on the online community, creating something new on their blogs, and searching for, synthesizing and disseminating information.

A behaviorist might call this objective fuzzy or unclear because the outcomes are not measurable, but we can argue that we know that the students have accomplished this task by looking at the links that they have added to their RSS feed, online reader, or their own blog. We could insist on a certain number of links, but doing so would undermine the objective by leading students to create a certain number of links rather than striving for quality of links. Therefore, quantifying the outcome is, perhaps, inappropriate.

However, we could argue that student ability to identify a good blog can be determined by looking at who else or how many other people with similar interests as the student have linked to the blog. In the world of participatory culture, success is determined by attention. Therefore, if a student has identified a particular blog as being helpful, and other people have linked to that blog as well, then there is some sense that the blog is meaningful. Of course, the teacher can conduct a qualitative assessment simply by talking to the student and asking him or her to explain the rationale for linking to that blog. That rationale can then be documented in the teacher's notes or even by the student on the blog.

Once we have an objective such as the one shown above, we can begin designing lessons with clarity and with the knowledge that we will be helping students not only identify the qualities of a good blog but also how to become a member of a community of interest or affinity group. Taking the time to do this taps into some of the skills that are needed within a participatory culture and thus adds a brick to the bridge over the participation gap experienced by some students.

FINAL WORDS

Teaching writing is challenging, which may be one reason why reading has typically held the lion's share of attention in teacher education and in national and state literacy efforts. However, the world of Web 2.0, participatory culture, and the lives of Generation 2.0 are making it clear that text production cannot be ignored. Young people are becoming more involved in using text to construct their own world, to build their identities, and to become members of far-flung communities. At the same time, facility with standard writing forms continues to be considered the measure of success in schools and in much of the workforce. As such, neither can be ignored as we work with Generation 2.0. The ideas suggested in this book are a step in bridging the participation gap in both academic and new literacies as well as an attempt to transcend the perceived chasm between in- and out-of-school literacies.

The ideas presented here are only a beginning; it is up to teachers to make it happen.

Part III

RESOURCES

New Literacies Questionnaire

This questionnaire is intended for teachers to use at the beginning of the year in order to discover student attitudes toward literacy and what they know about online media, digital technologies, and the new literacies. It is *not* a scientifically validated survey and should not be used as such. Teachers should feel free to add to or subtract from this survey as appropriate for their students and changing technologies. Teachers can administer this questionnaire using paper, but they are encouraged to use an online survey service such as SurveyMonkey or the "Form" tool in Google Documents.

Section 1: Describe yourself as a text user and creator.

	Not	*Somewhat*	*Confident*	*Mostly*	*Highly*
How confident are you as a reader?					
How confident are you as a writer?					
How confident are you as a computer user?					

1. What are your strengths as a writer? (open response)

2. Where do you think you need to improve as a writer? (open response)

3. What kind of writing do you do on your own? (open response)

4. What other kinds of texts (for example, podcasts, making beats, videos, fanfiction, mash-ups, anime, mixes and remixes, etc.) do you create? (open response)

Section 2: Describe your technology experience and knowledge.

_____ I own a computer that only I use.

_____ My family owns a computer that I share with other members of the family.

_____ I am able to use a computer at friends' homes.

_____ I regularly use a public computer at a library, community center, or other public location.

_____ I am taking (or have taken) one or more classes in a computer classroom.

_____ I use the Internet regularly.

	Never heard of it	*I did it in the past, but don't do it now*	*I use it once in a while*	*I use it all the time*	*If I had to, I could show someone how to do it*	*I have taught lots of people how to use it*
Social networking site (Facebook, MySpace, etc.)						
Web page						
Wiki (pbworks, wetpaint, wikispaces)						
Blog (livejournal, blogger, wordpress, etc.)						

	Never heard of it	I did it in the past, but don't do it now	I use it once in a while	I use it all the time	If I had to, I could show someone how to do it	I have taught lots of people how to use it
Word processor (Word)						
Spreadsheet (Excel)						
Presentation software (PowerPoint, Keynote, etc.)						
Video production (iMovie, Moviemaker, etc.)						
Soundmixing (Audacity, GarageBand)						
Photosharing (Flickr)						
Videosharing (YouTube)						
Music sharing						
Texting/SMS						
E-mail						
Instant messaging						
Gaming (independent game systems)						
Gaming (online)						
Cell phone						

These next questions can be used if you wish to develop an even deeper understanding of your students' use of digital technologies.

1. How many texts do you send each day? (estimate the number)

   1–5   6–10   11–15   16–30   31–50   More than 50

2. How many e-mails do you send each day? (estimate the number)

   1–5   6–10   11–15   16–30   31–50   More than 50

3. How much time do you spend on instant messaging each day?

   Less than 1 hour/day   2–3 hours/day   More than 3 hours/day

4. How often do you check your social networking page?

   1–3 times/day   3–5 times/day
   5–10 times/day   More than 10 times/day

5. What services do you have on your cell phone? List as many as you can think of. (open response)

6. What types of things do you use your cell phone for? List as many things as you can think of. (open response)

7. How much time do you spend listening to music each day?

   Less than 1 hour/day   1–2 hours/day
   3–5 hours/day   More than 5 hours/day

8. Do you own a television?

   Yes   No

9. How many hours of television do you watch?

   Less than 1 hour/day   2–3 hours/day   More than 3 hours/day

10. How many hours a day do you spend gaming?

    Less than 1 hour/day   2–3 hours/day   More than 3 hours/day

11. What other digital tools or ways of communicating and writing do you do that this questionnaire left out? (open response)

Recommended Reading

These books represent some of the recent work done in the field of the new litera-cies. Some focus on classroom practice and will help teachers plan instruction. Other books are more theoretical or research oriented and are suggested for readers who would like to do a deep dive into the issues of the new literacies. It is recommended that readers form collegial learning circles or book clubs to get the most out of the suggested texts and to develop ways of implementing what they learn into their teach-ing practices. Teachers can also explore the new literacies by using blogs, wikis, or other online media in conjunction with the reading groups.

Alvermann, D. (Ed.) (2010). *Adolescents' online literacies: Connecting classrooms, digital media, and popular culture.* New York: Peter Lang.

This edited collection includes contributions from some of the top researchers in youth and new literacies. The reader can learn more about the different types of new literacies that youth are engaging in by reading chapters on multimodal pedagogies, Webkinz, blogs, social networking, e-zines, hip hop, and video games.

Baron, N. (2008). *Always on: Language in an online and mobile world.* New York: Oxford University Press.

Baron provides a fascinating look at how language is changing as a result of digital technologies. She looks closely at specific aspects of language use, such as spelling, punctuation, and grammar, and offers insights into the relationship between language use and society. This book is useful for teachers interested in learning more about the specifics of language change and the Internet.

Davies, J., & Merchant, G. (2009). *Web 2.0 for schools: Learning and social partici-pation.* New York: Peter Lang.

Davies and Merchant discuss how to use Web 2.0 tools to enrich the learning of youth. The authors explore blogging, photo sharing, YouTube, music sharing, virtual worlds, and wikis as tools teachers can tap into as they work to engage students in authentic literacy practices.

Gee, J. P. (2003). *What video games have to teach us about literacy and learning.* New York: Palgrave Macmillan.

Although this is an older book, it is included here because Gee was one of the first literacy scholars to look seriously at the relationship of video games to learning. In this book, Gee examines the structure of video games and identifies a number of learning principles embedded in video games that can be useful when considering the design of intentional learning environments such as school. Teachers who wish to gain a better understanding of why many youth are so enamored by video games should read this book. This book is also useful for helping to dispel some of the negative myths around the gaming culture.

Gustavson, L. (2007). *Youth learning on their own terms: Creative practices and classroom teaching.* London: Routledge.

Through a close examination of the literacy practices of three youth, Gustavson provides the reader with a rich understanding of what the new literacies mean in today's world. Each case study is richly descriptive, and teachers will gain greater insights into the lives of youth who do not always excel in the classroom. The reader will walk away from this book with the sense that the literate lives of youth are much greater than the glimpses we get through school performances.

Herrington, A., Hodgson, K., & Moran, C. (2009). *Teaching the new writing: Technology, change, and assessment in the twenty-first-century classroom.* New York: Teachers College Press.

This edited collection contains contributions from teachers ranging from early childhood education to college. Each chapter offers a description of the digital writing assignments done in the author's classes, as well as a discussion of the assessments used to determine student learning.

Hicks, T. (2009). *The digital writing workshop.* Portsmouth, NH: Heinemann.

Hicks offers an easily accessible explanation of how to use today's technologies to develop writing workshops. As an experienced literacy educator, the author offers practical ideas for the teacher just beginning to think about how to move the writing workshop into the twenty-first century.

Ito, M., Horst, H., Bittanti, M., Boyd, D., Herr-Stephenson, B., Lange, P. G., et al. (2008). *Living and learning with new media: Summary of findings from the Digital Youth Project.* Boston: MIT Press.

This report (available free online and for purchase as a hard copy), summarizes the findings from the three-year study of a number of adolescents and young adults as they participated in a variety of digital practices. The pdf version of the report is available at digitalyouth.ischool.berkeley.edu/report. A two-page summary is also available. The results of the study are explored in detail in the book *Hanging Out, Messing Around, Geeking Out: Living and Learning with New Media*. The report explains why youth use online media and explores the implications for adult involvement. The authors also discuss issues of standardization in respect to online media. Any of these texts are useful for teachers looking to increase their knowledge of how young people are using online media and why those tools are so important to youth.

Lankshear, C., & Knobel, M. (2008). *New literacies: Everyday practices and classroom learning* (2nd ed.). New York: McGraw-Hill.

Lankshear and Knobel are two of the leaders in the scholarship of the new literacies. In this book they lead the reader through developing understandings of what the new literacies are and how the new literacies involve new ways of thinking and seeing the world, and then demonstrate what those concepts mean through explorations of blogging and remix. They then turn their attention to the implications of these practices for classroom instruction. Scholarly in scope and in writing style, this book is for teachers who are not afraid to grapple with big ideas.

Palfrey, J., & Gasser, U. (2008). *Born digital: Understanding the first generation of digital natives*. New York: Basic Books.

Palfrey and Gasser are legal scholars who provide a detailed look at the qualities of those youth called digital natives. The authors draw on their knowledge of law to discuss issues of privacy, copyright, and fair use in addition to explaining the unique nature of digital youth. Teachers will find this book especially useful for understanding the context of the world in which young people move.

Rosen, L. D. (2010). *Rewired: Understanding the igeneration and the way they learn*. New York: Palgrave Macmillan.

Rosen, a psychologist, uses easy-to-understand language to explain how the youth who have grown up in a digital world learn differently than those of previous generations. This book is a good entry-level text for those just learning about the relationship between the new literacies and their impact on youth and learning. Rosen also includes some concrete suggestions addressing the learning needs of youth.

Tapscott, D. (2009). *Grown up digital: How the net generation is changing your world*. New York: McGraw-Hill.

This book was inspired by the findings of a large-scale research project conducted by Tapscott and colleagues. The author leads the reader through an explanation of the qualities of the "net generation." He explores the myths and realities of the net generation and discusses how the changes being wrought by the net generation can be directed toward improving the world. Teachers will find the language in this book accessible and helpful for understanding why they are challenged by today's youth and what they can be working toward.

Thomas, A. (2007). *Youth online: Identity and literacy in the digital age.* New York: Peter Lang.

    Thomas's book offers a unique perspective into the new literacies, because her work involved youth from several countries, including the United States, England, Australia, and Holland. This book offers fascinating insights into the ways young people are using the new literacies. Although the book is research oriented and thus does not offer ideas for use in the classroom, teachers may find it a helpful tool for understanding the young people they work with on a daily basis.

Wilber, D. (2010). *iwrite: Using blogs, wikis, and digital stories in the English classroom.* Portsmouth, NH: Heinemann.

    Based on her extensive experience teaching reading and writing to adolescents as well as students who are just starting college, Wilber offers concrete ideas for using blogs, wikis, and digital stories for supporting the development of student reading and writing skills. The author also offers a clear description of the new literacies as well as the lives of those who have grown up with those literacies.

Williams, B. T. (2009). *Shimmering literacies: Popular culture and reading and writing online.* New York: Peter Lang.

    This book will be useful for anyone interested in learning more about how different aspects of popular culture support the literacies of young people. Williams discusses the role of audience and examines how youth are creating new forms and genres of text, how these new texts contribute to identify construction, and what these texts mean to youth, particularly in the realm of being pleasurable to engage in.

Reference List

Atwell, N. (1987/1998). *In the middle*. Portsmouth, NH: Heinemann.

Baron, D. (2001). From pencils to pixels: The stages of literacy technologies. In E. Cushman, E. R. Kintgen, B. M. Kroll, & M. Rose (Eds.), *Literacy: A critical sourcebook* (pp. 70–84). Boston: Bedford/St. Martin's.

Baron, N. (2008). *Always on: Language in an online and mobile world*. New York: Oxford University Press.

Bean, J. C., Drenk, D., & Lee, F. D. (1982). Microtheme strategies for developing cognitive skills. In C. W. Griffin (Ed.), *Teaching writing in all disciplines: New directions for teaching and learning* (pp. 27–38). San Francisco: Jossey-Bass.

Black, R. (2005). Access and affiliation: The literacy and composition practices of English-language learners in an online fanfiction community. *Journal of Adolescent & Adult Literacy, 49*(2), 118–128.

Bruns, A. (2008). *Blogs, Wikipedia, Second Life, and beyond: From production to produsage*. New York: Peter Lang.

Chandler-Olcott, K., & Mahar, D. (2003). Adolescents' anime-inspired "fanfiction": An exploration of multiliteracies. *Journal of Adolescent & Adult Literacy, 46*(7), 556–566.

Heath, S. B. (1982). What no bedtime story means: Narrative skills at home and school. *Language in Society, 11*, 49–76.

Heath, S. B. (1983). *Ways with words*. New York: Cambridge University Press.

Ito, M., Horst, H., Bittanti, M., Boyd, D., Herr-Stephenson, B., Lange, P. G., et al. (2008). *Living and learning with new media: Summary of findings from the Digital Youth Project*. Boston: MIT Press.

Jenkins, H., Clinton, K., Purushotma, R., Robinson, A. J., & Weigel, M. (2006). Confronting the challenges of participatory culture: Media education for the 21st century. Retrieved from www.digitallearning.macfound.org/site/c.enJLKQNlFiG/b.2108773/apps/nl/content2.asp?content_id=%7BCD911571-0240-4714-A93B-1D0C07C7B6C1%7D.

Lanham, R. (2006). *Revising prose* (5th ed.). New York: Longman.

Lankshear, C., & Knobel, M. (2008). *New literacies: Everyday practices and classroom learning* (2nd ed.). New York: McGraw-Hill.

Madden, M., & Smith, A. (2010). *Reputation management and social media.* Washington, DC: Pew Internet & American Life Project.

Mali, T. (2008). The the impotence of proofreading performance. Retrieved June 17, 2010, from www.youtube.com/watch?v=OonDPGwAyfQ.

Mali, T. (2009). The the impotence of proofreading. Retrieved June 17, 2010, from www.taylormali.com/index.cfm?webid=30.

McIntosh, J. (2009). What would Buffy do? Notes on Dusting Edward Cullen. Retrieved June 17, 2010, from www.wimnonline.org/WIMNsVoicesBlog/?p=1272.

National Commission on Writing. (2003). *The neglected "R": The need for a writing revolution.* New York: College Entrance Examination Board.

National Council of Teachers of English. (2008). The NCTE definition of 21st century literacies. Retrieved June 17, 2010, from www.ncte.org/positions/statements/21stcentdefinition.

O'Bryne, W. I. (2009). Facilitating critical thinking skills through online content creation. Retrieved June 17, 2010, from wiobryne.com/Personal_Site/Hoax_Websites.html.

Palfrey, J., & Gasser, U. (2008). *Born digital: Understanding the first generation of digital natives.* New York: Basic Books.

Plester, B., Wood, C., & Joshi, P. (2009). Exploring the relationship between children's knowledge of text message abbreviations and school literacy outcomes. *British Journal of Developmental Psychology, 27,* 145–161. doi: 10.1348/026151008X320507.

Roberts, D., Foehr, U., & Rideout, V. (2008). Trends in media use. *The Future of Children, 18*(1), 11–33.

Rogoff, B. (1990). *Apprenticeship in thinking.* New York: Oxford University Press.

Rogoff, B. (2003). *The cultural nature of human development.* New York: Oxford University Press.

Rosen, L. D. (2010). *Rewired: Understanding the igeneration and the way they learn.* New York: Palgrave Macmillan.

Squires, L. (2007). Whats the use of apostrophes? Gender difference and linguistic variation in instant messaging. AU TESOL Working Papers, 4. Retrieved from www1.american.edu/tesol/WorkingPapers04.html.

Vygotsky, L. S. (1978). *Mind in society.* Cambridge, MA: Harvard University Press.

Watson, J. M., & Strayer, D. L. (in press). Supertaskers: Profiles in extraordinary multitasking ability. *Psychonomic Bulletin & Review.*

Wohlwend, K. E. (2009). Early adopters: Playing new literacies and pretending new technologies in print-centric classrooms. *Journal of Early Childhood Literacy, 9*(2), 117–140.

Zar, J. (1992). Candidate for a Pullet Surprise. Retrieved June 17, 2010, from www.bios.niu.edu/zar/zar.shtml.

About the Author

Gloria E. Jacobs is associate professor of literacy education at St. John Fisher College, and she earned her PhD at the University of Rochester's Warner Graduate School of Education and Human Development. She has presented her work on adolescent literacy and technology at international and national conferences and has published her research in journals such as *Reading Research Quarterly*, *Journal of Literacy Research*, and *Journal of Adolescent and Adult Literacy.*